THE POCKET GUIDE TO
SEATTLE

Pocket Guide to Seattle — 5th Edition

Cover design by Magrit Baurecht
Cover illustration by Margaret Chodos-Irvine
Illustrations by E.B. "Pete" McLean

Library of Congress Cataloging in Publication Data
The pocket guide to seattle and surrounding areas.
    Includes index.
    96-060636
    ISBN 0-9621935-6-9
1. Seattle, Wash, — Guidebooks, 2. Seattle
Region (Wash.) — I. McLean, Duse, 1937-

The Pocket Guide to Seattle is a complete,
updated handbook for the Greater Seattle area.
For information about volume discounts or
special editions contact:

Thistle Press
P.O. Box 732
Bellevue, Washington 98009
Phone: 206 885-3173 Fax: 206 885-3666

Printed in the United States of America

THE POCKET GUIDE TO

SEATTLE

AND SURROUNDING AREAS

BY DUSE McLEAN

Thistle Press

PREFACE
TO THE FIFTH EDITION

Seattle is like a teenager — always growing and changing. In the 1980s it grew too fast and became too "in," and long-time residents felt unsettled. Then it slowed down too much, and everyone anguished over what was wrong. Now it seems to have its equilibrium — downtown is stable, but new buildings are opening and long-talked-about projects for the Watefront are finally being built. Maybe we can enjoy it for a while before the next phase starts.

With all its ups and downs, Seattle casts a spell over people, making them want to visit, stay longer, and know more. This new edition of *The Pocket Guide* covers present-day Seattle with its history and background to add to the reader's understanding. Thanks to help from knowledgeable locals, the popular Glossary section has been updated to include the latest vocabulary.

Along with the following acknowledgmnets, special thanks to Seattle for being such a great city to write about!

Acknowledgements

Thanks to the many people who helped with this fifth edition of *The Pocket Guide* — it would not have been possible without their help and support. The Visitor Information staff at the Seattle/King County Convention and Visitors Bureau always know what's going on in Seattle and are eager to share the latest news, as are hotel concierges. Thanks also to the hundreds of people who answered my questions when I called them.

The book's sharp new look, in honor of its fifth anniversary, is by graphic designer Magrit Baurecht, with a new cover illustration by Margaret Chodos-Irvine. Editor Elisa Hampton made sure there were no loose ends as she checked it all. Special thanks to my husband Pete, who did the book's illustrations as part of the family team that produced the first *Pocket Guide* and has contributed greatly to each new edition.

And thanks to you, my readers, who continue to make *The Pocket Guide* a success.

TABLE OF CONTENTS

PART II

AND MORE

MAPS

Seattle

INTRODUCTION

Seattle is a young city with a rich history. Founded by determined pioneers who envisioned a grand city in the rugged Northwest, Seattle has grown and prospered on the foundations they laid.

The first settlers, known as the Denny party, landed on Alki Point in West Seattle in November 1851. Finding the harbor better on Elliott Bay, they moved to the present site the following spring and named their city after Chief Sealth, the Suquamish Indian chief who had befriended them.

The city grew slowly at first, but with the arrival of the Great Northern train line in the 1880s, Seattle flourished. It suffered a temporary setback in 1889 when fire consumed most of the downtown area, but citizens quickly rebuilt. When gold was discovered in the Klondike in 1896 prospectors poured into Seattle to buy provisions for the trip north. Although the Klondike gold rush was short-lived, it created many fortunes in Seattle.

Seattle's first commercial ventures in the 1850s were lumber, fishing, and shipping, most in trade with a booming San Francisco. These same industries continue to be important to this day, although now much of the commerce moves between Seattle and Asia. With 80,000 employees, Boeing is still the state's biggest employer, while a flourishing computer industry continues to grow on the east side of Lake Washington. The city now has about 530,000 people, while the greater Seattle/Puget Sound area has over two million.

For many years Seattle was known as the Queen City because of its dominance in King County and the Northwest, but in 1982 the Seattle/King County Convention and Visitors Bureau sponsored a contest for a new, more contemporary nickname. The winning entry, The Emerald City, proclaimed, "Seattle is the jewel of the Northwest, the Queen of the Evergreen State, and is the many-faceted city of space, elegance, magic, and beauty." Public art abounds, thanks to Seattle's 1% for Art program which designates one percent of certain City Capital Improvement Program funds for artworks.

In addition to its remarkable physical beauty, Seattle is known for its climate. The lush green hills and gardens are a result of seasonal, gentle rains brought by Pacific air currents. The resulting maritime climate keeps Seattle's temperatures moderate — it rarely freezes or snows in the winter and days are mild in the summer. Although it has a reputation for being a rainy city, Seattle's average annual rainfall is 35 to 37 inches, less than many East Coast cities. The rainy season, November through April, brings short, gray days of fog, mist and light rain. Daytime temperatures in the winter months are typically in the 40s or 50s and seldom drop below freezing. The long days of the summer months are usually dry and sunny with high temperatures in the 70s or low 80s. A raincoat or jacket usually is enough in winter and a lightweight jacket or sweater is a good idea in the summer.

GETTING AROUND

Seattle's downtown is a narrow area about two miles long, bounded by the Kingdome and the International District on the south and Seattle Center to the north, and confined by Elliott Bay on the west and I-5 to the east (see map on page 145). Within this small area are the major business buildings, hotels, and shops, including Pioneer Square and the Pike Place Market. Metro buses are free downtown between 6am and 7pm, providing a perfect way to sightsee. Note: Seattle police enforce the no-jaywalking law; a ticket for jaywalking costs $38.

Avenues run north to south; streets run east and west. Addresses will include north/south, east/west designations, which are crucial to finding the right address. The basic number-grid system extends throughout the greater Seattle area.

Free maps of the downtown area are available from several places, including the **Visitor Information Center** operated by the Seattle/King County Convention and Visitors Bureau on the Galleria level of the Washington State Convention and Trade Center; the Visitor Center on the main floor of Westlake Center; the Information booth at the Pike Place Market; and from concierges at most hotels. There are also computerized information kiosks in several locations in town and at the airport.

Metered parking is available on the streets; no-parking hours depend upon locations. Most of the parking lots are privately owned and rates may vary widely; check around a little before parking. Currently, most lots charge between $3-$6 for two hours. For less expensive parking try lots by the Kingdome at the south end of town or by Seattle Center to the north and take public transportation around downtown.

METRO

Metro buses are free from 6am to 7pm in the downtown Ride Free Zone (also known as the Magic Carpet), which extends from First Avenue to Sixth Avenue or the I-5 freeway between Jackson on the south and Bell on the north. It makes a walking tour of the city easy — just hop on a free bus when you're tired. Buses in the Metro underground tunnel between Olive and Ninth Avenue on the north, and Jackson and Fifth Avenue on the south end, are always free but have restricted hours: 5am-7pm, weekdays; 10:30am-

5:30pm Saturdays; closed Sundays. Metro system maps are available in the Metro information Center in the tunnel at Westlake Center and at Metro offices in the Exchange Building at Second Avenue and Marion (see the ornate gilded lobby even if you don't need a pass). Most bus stops have route maps and schedules for the buses using that stop; schedules are available in many downtown banks, hotels, office buildings and the Seattle Public Library. Several types of passes are available: on Saturdays, Sundays and holidays a $1.70 all-day pass may be purchased on the buses. A Regional Reduced Fare Permit is available for disabled and senior citizens; call 553-3060 for information. Metro's information line operates 24 hours a day.

Hours:	Vary with routes.
Cost:	One zone, $.85 non-peak; $1.10 peak hours. Two zones, $1.10 non-peak; $1.60 peak hours. Peak hours are 6am-9am & 3pm-6pm. Exact change required.
Phone:	553-3000 for route and schedule information

THE WATERFRONT STREETCAR

Metro's vintage Australian streetcars run along Alaskan Way on the Waterfront from Pier 70 at the north end to South Main Street on the south, making several stops along the way. The line turns onto South Main Street and continues east to Fifth Avenue South and South Jackson Street, across the street from the transit tunnel. A ticket is good for 1½ hours, allowing passengers to get off and on for sightseeing. Metro passes are accepted. Streetcars come every 20 to 30 minutes.

Hours:	7am-6:15pm weekdays; 10:30am-6:30pm weekends. 7:15am-11pm summer.

Cost:	One zone: $.85 non-peak, $1.10 peak hours.
Phone:	553-3000 (Metro)

THE MONORAIL

The Monorail, built for the 1962 World's Fair, travels between downtown Seattle and Seattle Center. It departs every 15 minutes from the Monorail station on the third floor of Westlake Center and takes two minutes to go the 1.2 miles to Center House near the Space Needle. Or, catch it at the Seattle Center terminal and ride to downtown.

Hours:	9am-11pm daily.
Cost:	Each way: Adults $1. Seniors & handicapped $.50. Children 5-12, $.75. Children under 5 free.
Phone:	441-6038 684-8582 (recording)

TAXIS

Taxis are available at major destinations and hotels. They may be flagged down in some areas, but are restricted as to where they may stop. It's usually best to call. Standard rates are set by the Taxi Commission: a trip from the airport to downtown costs about $30 for a taxi, slightly more for a limousine. A trip within the downtown area will cost $5 to $10 depending on distance. Farwest, Orange and Yellow Cabs are the major companies and there are many small companies.

HOW TO USE THIS GUIDE

The Pocket Guide is organized from the point of view of someone starting out to see Seattle from downtown; all directions, travel times and distances originate from central downtown. Phone numbers are local for most areas unless otherwise stated; all long distance numbers require an area

code — in Seattle the area code is 206; in outlying areas the area code is 360.

This book is divided into four major sections.
The first three are grouped by their proximity to
downtown Seattle: The "Downtown" section covers places easily accessible by public transportation or walking; the "In and Around" area is a
little farther out — a 20- to 30-minute drive from
downtown and accessible by Metro buses; the
"Out and About" destinations are half-day or
longer excursions and most require a car. The last
section, "And More," has listings by special interests, such as ferries, museums and sports, which
are of interest to Seattle residents and visitors
alike. **Unless noted, all places are handicapped
accessible**. **Boldfaced** items are referenced in the
index.

Please note: We have checked all listed hours,
costs, and phone numbers for accuracy but know
that inevitably some will change after publication.
Some attractions operate on a limited schedule or
not at all during the winter. **Please call to verify
days and hours of operation when planning
your schedule.** Prices quoted are the standard,
published prices and include tax. Most attractions
offer off-season or group discounts; it pays to ask.
Many have special events throughout the year.

The Pocket Guide to Seattle includes hundreds
of places in the greater Seattle area, from the best
known to favorite hideaways. It has been com-
pletely rewritten and updated with current information for this edition. We have not received
favors or promotional fees from attractions. If
we've missed any of our readers' favorites, please
write and tell us about it:

Pocket Guide to Seattle
c/o Thistle Press
P.O. Box 732
Bellevue, WA 98009

PART I

DOWNTOWN

Downtown Seattle is dramatic. Steep hills, stunning views between buildings, and classic early 20th century structures mingled with striking new skyscrapers make the downtown area exhilarating. The bustling retail area stretches from the large stores by Westlake Park to the smaller specialty shops along the streets and in office towers to the south. Bounded by the freeway on the east and water on the west, the narrow downtown area extends two miles, from the Kingdome on the south side of Pioneer Square to Seattle Center on the north. Avenues run roughly north and south, parallel to the water; streets run east-west, up steep hills in the middle of town.

The best way to see downtown is on foot. There are courtyards, lobbies and shops to poke-into — in lovely turn-of-the century, art deco and modern buildings — and views to pause over, with public art sprinkled throughout. Best of all, with Metro's free transportation, there's always a free bus on the street or in the Tunnel to rescue the weary.

It's possible to see everything in this section in one day if you don't pause long at any place or succumb to a ferry ride or shopping. It would be much better to savor the city and spend time enjoying it, perhaps combining something from the Downtown section with a destination from the In and Around section.

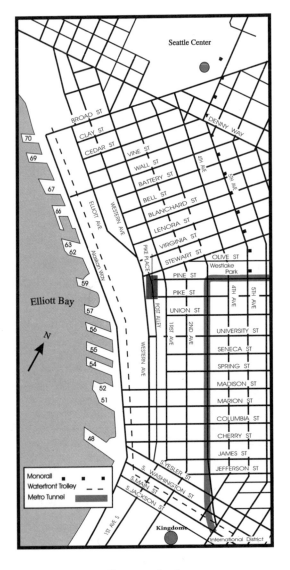

Downtown Seattle

PIKE PLACE MARKET

Known as the heart and soul of Seattle, the Pike Place Market has been a Seattle institution since it opened in 1907. Started because housewives wanted to save money by buying directly from producers, it is the oldest continuously operating farmers' market in the United States.

After thriving during its first three decades, the Market declined during the middle years of this century. City officials wanted to replace it with high-rise condos and office buildings, but a citizens' campaign mounted in the 1970s saved it. Tiles with contributors' names pave the floor of the main Market building. A recent fundraising campaign has added fish on stairway walls, pig hoof prints on the sidewalk, and brass fish wrapped around columns, all with their donors'

Post Alley in Pike Place Market

names. It's a great place to go if you're hungry, looking for local color, something unusual, good views, or just looking.

The **Pike Place Preservation and Development Association (PDA)** offers health and social services such as low-income housing, a senior center, child care, and counseling to area residents. **Rachel**, the life-sized bronze piggy bank located under the Market's landmark clock, collects contributions for PDA projects.

The Market includes several buildings on Pike Place, Post Alley and First Avenue between Union and Virginia Streets. In addition to meat, fish and produce stalls, it has arts and crafts, flowers, bakeries, small restaurants, entertainers, and a theater. The daystall merchants change from day to day, but the other stalls, including the warren of shops on the lower floors, are permanent merchants.

The highstalls on the main level with their dazzling displays of fish and produce are long-time Market tenants who always occupy the same spaces. The lowstall merchants to the north vie for space daily according to their places in the hierarchy. These merchants sell only locally produced merchandise.

The best way to see the Market is on foot. (It is wheelchair accessible, but crowds make the going difficult.) Take a bus or park in nearby lots on Western Avenue or along the waterfront under the **Alaskan Way Viaduct**. Stairs, known as the **Pike Place Hillclimb**, connect the Market to the waterfront below. There is an elevator located a little north of the stairs in the Market but it is not easy to find; there is also an elevator on the Hillclimb side of the street south of the stairs. Two restrooms are located on the lower floor of the main building.

An Information Booth, located on the corner of Pike Place and First Avenue near the clock, also sells discounted tickets to some events. They have Market maps with information about merchants and shops and will store packages for shoppers on a space-available basis. They also have a self-guided tour map and a brochure listing restaurants in the Market. Market restaurants may open earlier or stay open later than general Market hours. Lowstalls generally don't open until 10am. For specific merchants, see listings in the phone book under Pike Place Market or call the Market.

The PDA holds a Market Classroom highlighting seasonal specialities or special events Saturday mornings from 9-10:30, or Wednesdays in the summer. Reservations required; phone 682-7453.

PIKE PLACE MARKET

Hours: 9am-6pm Mon-Sat; 11am-5pm Sun. Restaurants have different hours. Some shops and stalls are not open on Sundays.

Phone: 682-7453

Rachel, the Market's life-sized piggy bank

THE WATERFRONT

Seattle has many fresh-water and salt-water waterfronts, but "The Waterfront" refers to the one and one-half mile stretch along **Alaskan Way** between Pier 48 at Main Street on the south end and Pier 70 at Broad Street on the north. The **Waterfront Streetcar** (page 6) serves the area, making several stops along Alaskan Way (which got its name because of the commerce from the docks to Alaska that started with the Klondike goldrush in the 1890s).

The piers, originally built at the turn of the century, are full of restaurants featuring fresh Northwest seafood, souvenir shops packed full of treasures, public art and many attractions. Tour boats, the Washington State Ferries, the Victoria Line, and the Victoria Clipper docks are located on Alaskan Way. Plaques along the way note historic events in Seattle's history.

Starting from the south end of the Waterfront, **Pier 48** at the foot of Main Street is across the street from the Waterfront Trolley stop. On the south side of the terminal building the Port of Seattle has placed three large periscopes so visitors can have a close-up view of the Port's container terminals. Go during working hours to see the port in action. Seattle is one of the largest container ports in the country and one of the busiest ports on the West Coast due to its deep water harbor and its proximity to Asia. The ***Royal Victorian*** sails daily to and from Victoria from the north side of the dock (page 70).

The small park north of Pier 48 has a totem pole and a public dock. The park, officially known as Alaska Square, is dedicated by the Port of Seattle to "the tremendous importance of Alaska to its southern seaport, Seattle."

Walking along Alaskan Way heading north, you will come next to the cupola at the foot of Washington Street. A plaque marks the last resting spot of the sidewheel steamer *Idaho*, a wayside mission hospital ship that sank in the harbor and was buried when the harbor was filled in. A little farther along, at the foot of Yesler Way, marks the spot where Henry Yesler built Seattle's first sawmill in 1852.

Pier 50 is the **Washington State Ferry** dock for passenger ferries to Vashon Island and Bremerton; **Pier 52** next door is the car ferry dock for boats going to Bainbridge Island (Winslow) and Bremerton (see Ferries, pages 98-100).

Continuing northbound, on the south side of **Pier 54** is the **Seattle Fire Department's waterfront station** where Seattle's two venerable fireboats, the *Alki* and the *Chief Seattle*, are moored. It's a rare treat to catch them in action in Elliott Bay. Two vintage fire engines are on display afternoons and evenings.

Hours: 1pm-5pm & 7pm-9pm.

Pier 54 houses **Ye Olde Curiosity Shop**, where bizarre artifacts and antiques are displayed along with souvenir items for sale, and **Ivar's Restaurant**, known for its clams and photographs of early Seattle. A statue of Ivar feeding seagulls is on the sidewalk.

Pier 54 has several options for sightseeing: When the weather is nice, bicycles may be rented to see the streets and kayaks to explore the shore from close to the water with a guide. The tall ship, *The Lady Washington* also departs from Pier 54;

The Waterfront: Alaskan Way and Washington Street

(see page 20). There are float planes for 20-minute up-in-the-air sightseeing trips; and fishing boats to find out what's under the water; call 623-6364.

Horse-drawn carriage tours of the Waterfront area may be picked up at Pier 54 and 55. To book a tour ahead of time, call **Sealth Horse Carriages**, 277-8282.

Pier 55 has several shops inside, great for browsing, with a Red Robin restaurant at the end. Boats for **Tillicum Village** and **Argosy** share dock space between Piers 55 and 56 (see page 21).

Trident Imports and Elliott's restaurant with its inviting outdoor tables and hanging flower baskets occupy Pier 56. The *Obsession* sails from the north side of the dock (see page 23).

Pier 57, known as **The Bay Pavilion**, has several shops and restaurants, public restrooms, and a gleaming classic carousel that operates daily in the summer and most days in the winter; rides cost $1.00. During the summer parasailing trips originate here and there are jazz concerts on Saturday afternoons (call 623-8600 for information).

The benches in the brick-lined **Waterfront Park** between Pier 57 and Pier 59 are good spots to pause and watch the ferries, tankers, and tugboats with their barges as they work on Elliott Bay. The park also has a statue of Christopher Columbus and a fountain. For a better view there are coin-operated telescopes along the sidewalk and at the ends of the piers. West Seattle and **Alki Point,** where Seattle's first pioneers settled in 1851, are visible across the bay.

THE AQUARIUM

The Seattle Aquarium is in the center of the Waterfront on **Pier 59** at the foot of the **Pike Place Hillclimb**. Exhibits focus on the Pacific marine habitat including seals and playful otters, an outstanding coral reef, and an overhead glass-domed underwater room that surrounds viewers with Northwest marine life. It also has a hands-on Discovery Lab and Tidepool exhibit, a salmon ladder and environmental information. Docents are usually available to answer questions, or visitors may rent an audiotape and hear Aquarium biologists talk about the exhibits. Hint: It can be cool inside. Food not allowed, none for sale; two restrooms inside the main building.

Hours:	10am-5pm, daily. 10am-7pm, summer.
Cost:	Adults $7.15. Seniors $5.70. Youths 6-18, $4.70. Children 3-5, $2.45. Under 2 free.
Phone:	386-4320

OMNIDOME FILM EXPERIENCE

The Omnidome shares **Pier 59** with the Aquarium. The theater features glorious nature films such as "The Eruption of Mount St. Helens" and "The Living Sea" on its 180-degree curved dome movie screen. There are restrooms and a refreshment stand in the lobby and Steamer's restaurant outside. A combination ticket for both the Omnidome and Aquarium is available.

Hours:	10am-5:30pm, daily; 10am-9:30pm, summer & weekends. Admission every half hour between movies.
Cost:	Adults $6.95. Youths 13-18 & seniors $5.95. Children 3-12, $4.95. Under 3 free. Second feature is $3.
Phone:	622-1869, 622-1868 (recording)

A restaurant, gift shop and public restrooms are also on Pier 59

Continuing north, Piers 62 and 63 are used for summer concerts while awaiting new harborfront plans. The Port's new **Bell Harbor Pier**, which includes the marina, a large public plaza with a fish fountain, **Anthony's restaurants**, and a fish cannery with windows for visitors, has filled in **Pier 66**. The complex will include the **International Conference Center** and **Odyssey Maritime Museum**.

Built for the 1962 World's Fair, the **Edgewater** on Pier 67 has been the only hotel on the Waterfront. The white building at **Pier 69** houses the **Port of Seattle** headquarters. In addition to its extensive waterfront activities, the Port also runs **Sea-Tac Airport, Fishermen's Terminal,** and the pleasure boat marina at **Shilshole**. Pier 69 is also home of the *Victoria Clipper* catamarans, which commute to Victoria (see page 70).

Pier 70, at the north end of the Waterfront, was built in 1901 for the large ships of the time and later was used to store canned salmon. The pier now holds Pier I Imports and other shops, and restaurants with terrific views. A public parking lot is upstairs. *Spirit of Puget Sound* cruises depart from the north side (see page 23).

The northern terminus of the **Waterfront Streetcar** is across the street from Pier 70 (see page 6). **Myrtle Edwards Park,** with its jogging trail, stretches one and a half miles north along the waterfront, ending at the public fishing dock and Elliott Bay Park at Pier 86.

HARBOR TOURS

Several harbor tour companies offer narrated views of Seattle's busy waterfront. All boats have enclosed seating areas for passengers wanting to stay inside and are handicapped accessible, although the ramps may be steep at low tide. Note: In addition to their scheduled tours, each company can accommodate groups for special occasions; call for information.

■ LADY WASHINGTON

A replica of Captain Gray's square rigger that was the first American ship to explore the Northwest, this ship offers 2-hour sails (the sunset sail is 3 hours) during the summer from Pier 54.

Hours	10am, 1, 3:30 and 6:30pm
Price:	Adults $20-$35.
	Seniors $18-$31.50.
	Children 5-12 $12.50-$26.
	Prices vary with times.
Phone:	682-4876

■ KAYAK SEATTLE

For a more intimate look at the Waterfront, Kayak Seattle has 1½ hour guided tours from their double sea kayaks.

Hours:	10, 11:30, 1, 2:30, & 4pm June-Sept, 7pm weekends.
Cost:	$35.00, children 8-12, $30.00.
Phone:	623-6364

Argosy and **Tillicum Village** Tours share space between **Pier 55** and **Pier 56.** Argosy has several tours on Puget Sound and Lake Washington.

■ HARBOR CRUISE

Boats cruise around Elliott Bay for a one-hour fact-filled tour. The narration covers Seattle's water-based history and its lively harbor scene. Snacks and beverages are available on board.

Hours:	Daily 2:45pm; plus April-Oct 12:15, 1:30, 2:45, & 4pm, with tours added in summer at 11am & 5:15pm.
Cost:	Adults $14.46.
	Children 5-12, $7.
	Under 5 free.
Phone:	623-4252

■ TILLICUM VILLAGE TOURS

Tillicum Tours combines a marine tour with a Northwest Indian salmon bake. Boats depart from Pier 55-56 and, after a narrated tour around Elliott

Bay, pass by Alki Point and cross Puget Sound to **Blake Island** Marine State Park. A salmon dinner is served in their cedar longhouse followed by a program of Northwest Coast Indian dances. There is time to see a movie about early Northwest Indian life, observe Indian artisans at work, visit the gift shop, or walk the island's natural forests and beaches.

Tours take four hours, including the 45-minute boat trip each way. Beverages of all types are available for purchase on the boat but no alcoholic beverages are served on the island.

Hours:	11:00am Sat all year; 11:00am Sat & Sun, Mar-Nov plus 6:30pm, May-Oct.; plus 4:30pm daily in summer. Call to verify & for reservations.
Cost:	Adults $54.37. Seniors $50.31. Teens $35.17. Children 6-12, $21.64. Toddlers 4-5, $10.82.
Phone:	443-1244

■ LOCKS CRUISE

Argosy's Locks Cruise at **Pier 57** is the most extensive of the water sightseeing tours. The tour begins with a brief cruise around Elliott Bay, then goes out into Puget Sound and heads north, travels through the locks, and docks at Chandler's Cove on Lake Union where passengers are bused back to downtown Seattle. The reverse tour is also available. Deli-type food and beverages may be purchased on board.

Hours:	10am, 1, 4, & 7pm June-Sept; plus 11:30am & 2:30pm in July & Aug. Call for schedule.
Cost:	Adults $22.61. Children 5-12, $12.06. Under 5 free.
Phone:	623-4252

■ SAIL SEATTLE

The *Obsession*, a 70-foot racing yacht, takes visitors out for a sail — or if there's no wind, a cruise — daily from May 1 to October 15. Afternoon trips are 1½ hours, evening sunset trips are 2½ hours.

Hours:	11am, 1:30pm, & 3pm, days. 6pm evenings.
Cost:	Days: Adults $20. Seniors $18. Under 12, $15. Evenings: Adults $35. Seniors $32. Under 12, $28.
Phone:	624-3931

■ THE VICTORIA CLIPPER

Weekends from June 21 to September 14 the *Victoria Clipper* has two-hour Sunset Cruises.

Hours:	7:30pm, June 21-Aug10. 6:45pm, Aug 16-Sept 14.
Cost:	Adults $16. Children $8.
Phone:	448-5000

■ THE SPIRIT OF PUGET SOUND

The sleek *Spirit of Puget Sound* on the north side of Pier 70 has daily lunch and dinner buffet cruises around the sound with on-board entertainment. Lunch cruises are two hours; dinner, three hours. Reservations recommended.

Hours:	Lunch: noon, daily except Sunday. Dinner: 7pm; Sun., 6pm
Cost:	Lunch $30. Dinner $52.85 (higher on weekends). Children under 12, half-price. Prices include tax and tips.
Phone:	443-1442

PIONEER SQUARE

Pioneer Square is where Seattle's settlers built their homes and businesses. At the south end of downtown, it includes the area roughly between Cherry and King Streets and from the waterfront east to Second or Third Avenues. The turn-of-the-century brick buildings replaced the original wooden buildings destroyed in the **Great Seattle Fire** in 1889. Seattle was in the midst of a boom and the merchants rushed to rebuild. To prevent another fire the city required that new buildings had to be built of brick, stone or metal. Most of the buildings were constructed between 1889 and 1896, giving the area an architecturally harmonious feeling.

Following World War I, many businesses left the area and moved northward. **Skid Road**, now **Yesler Way,** which pioneers had used to slide (or "skid") logs down to Henry Yesler's mill on the waterfront, came to be synonymous with the down-and-out people who remained in the area. After several decades of neglect, Pioneer Square was rediscovered in the 1960s and 1970s and the handsome buildings were restored for shops and offices.

The broad, tree-lined sidewalks make browsing along the shops delightful. Art galleries, antique shops, boutiques, theaters, bookstores and restaurants are nestled in this area. There are small parks and sidewalk cafes to enjoy in good weather.

Like **Pike Place Market**, Pioneer Square is an officially designated historical district. Brochures for self-guided walking tours are available at shops in the area.

UNDERGROUND TOUR

The Underground Tour, an informative, light-hearted history of Seattle and the Pioneer Square area, begins with a half-hour introduction followed by a guided walking tour of the area. When Seattle rebuilt after the fire, it kept the original

sea-level streets, even though they flooded with in-
coming tides. Several years later the city raised
the streets 10-15 feet, thereby burying the lower
floors of buildings. The Underground Tour covers
area history both above and below ground.

Tours start at **Doc Maynard's Public House**
near the totem pole in **Pioneer Square Park** on
First Avenue between Cherry and James. Hint:
Some walkways and stairs have uneven surfaces;
not wheelchair accessible; no restrooms on tour.

Hours:	11am, 1 & 3pm daily, plus others added in July & Aug. Call for schedule.
Cost:	Adults $6.50. Seniors $5.50. Students 13-17, $5. Children 6-12, $2.75.
Phone:	682-4646

The white terra-cotta **Smith Tower** on the
corner of Second Avenue and Jefferson, built in
1914, was for many years the tallest building west
of the Mississippi. The ornate **Chinese Room** on
the tower's 35th floor is open to the public. Visitors can walk around its outside balcony and see
how Seattle developed below. Access is by one
of the gleaming antique brass elevators.

SMITH TOWER TOURS

Hours:	10am-7pm daily. Call to verify.
Cost:	Adults $2. Children & Seniors $1.
Phone:	622-4004

KLONDIKE GOLD RUSH NATIONAL PARK
17 South Main Street

One of the treasures in Pioneer Square is the
tiny Klondike Gold Rush National Park Visitor
Center, which is not really a park but a one-room
museum in a small Pioneer Square building. The
Center is filled with historical information about

the Klondike Gold Rush, which was set off when the steamer *Portland* docked in Seattle in 1897 carrying the legendary ton of gold from the Klondike. The park rangers will demonstrate gold-panning techniques and show movies about Seattle's development and its role in the Gold Rush.

Hours:	9am-5pm, daily.
Cost:	Free.
Phone:	553-7220

WATERFALL PARK
2nd Avenue & Main

Another jewel is the almost hidden Waterfall Garden, built and maintained by the Annie E. Casey Foundation in honor of United Parcel Service employees. The Casey family founded the UPS company on this spot in 1907. In addition to its 22-foot man-made waterfall, it has sheltered tables and lush garden plantings.

Hours:	Daily, 10am-5pm; summer, 10am-6pm.

Across the street at Second Avenue and Main Street is a fire station with public restrooms on the Main Street side.

INFORMATION BOOTH

Volunteers from the Assistance League of Seattle staff an information booth located on Occidental Avenue and Main Street. Open only in the summer.

Hours:	10:30am-3:00pm Tues.-Sat., June 1-Sept. 1.

King Street marks the southern border of the Pioneer Square area. The **King Street Station** at Fourth Avenue and King Street is used by **Amtrak** trains. The **Waterfront Streetcar** and the **Metro Tunnel** terminate at Fifth and Jackson, across the street from one another. **The Kingdome** and its parking lots are between Occidental and Second Avenue, off King Street.

Getting to Pioneer Square:

By car: Drive south on First, Second, or Third Avenues; there are many parking lots near the Kingdome; prices vary.

By bus: Take a bus heading south on First Avenue and get off near Yesler Street by the pergola or, in the tunnel, at either the Pioneer Square or International District station. Or take the Waterfront Streetcar heading south and get off at Occidental Park. Call Metro, 553-3000, for information.

Pioneer Square

THE KINGDOME

The Kingdome is the massive concrete mushroom on the south side of Pioneer Square. Officially known as the **King County Stadium**, it is where the **Seahawks** (football) and **Mariners** (baseball) play their games. Its self-supporting concrete roof, the world's largest, allows unobstructed views for everyone. Completed in 1976 for $57 million, and recently remodelled for almost as much, the Kingdome can hold up to 65,000 people in the dome and the new exhibition center for trade shows, concerts and special events. Tickets for Kingdome events may be purchased at the box office or through **Ticketmaster**, 628-0888.

Tours are available, depending upon event scheduling, and may include a team practice. The souvenir shop/**sports museum** is open during tours and events. Tours meet at Gate D and exit at Gate B; they take about an hour.

KINGDOME TOURS

Hours:	Call for times & reservations.
Cost:	Adults & teens $4. Seniors & children $2.
Phone:	296-3128

Getting to the Kingdome:

By car: Drive south on First, Second or Third Avenues, or along Alaskan Way. Parking: There are many lots near the Kingdome; prices vary.

By bus: Take a bus heading south on First Avenue or a bus in the Tunnel to the International District stop. Extra buses are added for special events. Or take the **Waterfront Streetcar** to either the Occidental Park or the King Street stop. Call **Metro**, 553-3000, for information.

THE INTERNATIONAL DISTRICT

The International District, also known as Chinatown, is the heart of Seattle's large Asian community. It covers the blocks east of the railroad tracks to the I-5 freeway and is bounded by Yesler on the north and Dearborn on the south. Look for the distinctive Asian street lights. The only area in the continental United States where Chinese, Japanese, Filipinos and other Asians have formed one neighborhood, its cultural diversity, art and architecture are best seen by walking.

The view of Elliott Bay from **Kobe Terrace Park** at the top of South Washington Street is spectacular. The park's centerpiece, the **10-ton Japanese lantern,** was given to Seattle by her sister city, Kobe, Japan. The park lies just above the **Nippon Kan Theatre** and the hillside **Danny Woo International District Community Garden** where neighborhood residents grow traditional fruits and vegetables.

Down the hill, Jackson Street, King Street and the side streets are lined with stores, businesses and restaurants. Note the historic tong and family association buildings with ornate balconies on the top floors. The **Chinese Bulletin Board** around the corner from King Street on Maynard Alley continues to function as a communications center for the neighborhood. The unique character of the neighborhood is reflected in **Hing Hay Park** with its red pavilion and dragon mural, the sculpture by George Tsutakawa up the street on Maynard, and the playground equipment designed by his son Gerard. **Uwajimaya's**, a combination department store, restaurant and grocery store, is filled with Asian delicacies and is one of the largest Japanese stores in North America.

There are many excellent restaurants featuring the various Asian cuisines; try dim sum and peek under all the lids. The **Chinatown Discovery Tour**, a walking tour of the area, includes dim sum on some of its tours (phone 236-0657).

Exhibits in the **Wing Luke Museum** trace the history of the International District, while the permanent exhibit "One Song, Many Voices" covers the history and culture of Asian Pacific Americans in Washington. In addition, there is work by local artists, historical displays, Asian folk art and a gift shop. The museum also has general information about the International District.

WING LUKE ASIAN MUSEUM

407 7th Avenue South

Hours:	11am-4:30pm Tues.-Fri. Noon-4pm Sat. & Sun.
Cost:	Adults $2.50. Seniors & students, $1.50. Children 5-12, $.75. Free Thursdays.
Phone:	623-5124

Getting to the International District

Driving: Go south on Fifth Avenue to Jackson Street; there are parking lots in the International District or near the Kingdome.

By bus: The **Ride Free Area** extends up Jackson Street to the freeway at Ninth Avenue and includes the International District. The Underground bus tunnel begins at Fifth Avenue and Jackson. Call Metro, 553-3000, for information.

The **Waterfront Streetcar's** southern terminus at Fifth Avenue South and Jackson and the last Metro Tunnel stop are across the street from the International District.

SEATTLE CENTER

Seattle Center, at the north end of downtown, was the site of the **1962 World's Fair** and is now an urban park. Located in the area known as the Denny Regrade, the 74-acre grounds are filled with art, gardens and fountains, shops, and restaurants, as well as the Pacific Science Center, the Space Needle and the city's cultural facilities.

Seattle's symbol, the 605-foot **Space Needle**, is located near the corner of Fifth Avenue and Broad Street. Built by private citizens who wanted an eye-catching symbol for the World's Fair, the Space Needle offers one of the best views of Seattle and Puget Sound. The Observation Deck at the top level (520 feet) has information about sights below and in the distance. There are two restaurants on the rotating level just below. One is more elegant (expensive) than the other, but both have the same outstanding view. The elevator ride is free for restaurant patrons. Both restaurants are very popular; to be sure of getting in, make reservations: (443-2100). There is a small cocktail lounge on the observation deck level; the elevator ride is not free for that. The 100-foot level is used for meetings and private parties. On both the ground and the observation levels there are gift and souvenir shops; minimal restroom facilities on the ground level.

THE SPACE NEEDLE
OBSERVATION DECK

The elevator ride to the observation deck at the top of the Space Needle takes 43 seconds.

Hours:	8am-midnight (varies with seasons & weekends).
Cost:	Adults $8.50. Seniors $7. Children 5-12, $4. Under 5 free. $1 discount at non-peak times: 8-10am & 8pm-midnight. Free with a restaurant reservation.
Phone:	443-2100

For those truly committed to the view, there is an annual pass for $49; call 443-9700.

THE MONORAIL

The Monorail terminal is across from the Space Needle entrance and is also accessible from inside Center House (see below). The Monorail shuttles between the downtown station in Westlake Center and Seattle Center every 10-15 minutes. The trip takes two minutes.

Cost: Each way:
       Adults $1. Seniors $.50.
       Children 5-12, $.75.
       Under 5 free.

Phone: 441-6038

INFORMATION

Seattle Center Information: The staff at the information desk on the main floor in Center House has information about Seattle Center events as well as general community information.

Phone: 684-7200, or
        684-8582 (recording)

The **Visitor Information Booth**, in the blue kiosk across from the **Monorail** ramp, is staffed by the knowledgeable people of the Seattle/King County Convention and Visitors Bureau. Maps of the Seattle Center grounds are available at both places.

Hours: 10am-6pm daily from
        Memorial Day to Labor Day.

Phone: 461-5854

CENTER HOUSE

The large building west of the Monorail and the Space Needle is Center House. Built as an armory in 1939, its recent remodel has made it brighter and more cheerful. (Note the art deco eagles over the lower back doorway on the

stadium side.) Used as the **Food Circus** during
the World's Fair, the center court is ringed with
food and gift shops. The restaurants are primarily
ethnic fast-food places; a few serve alcoholic beverages. It's a good place to go when everyone
wants something different to eat. Gift shops are
on the main and top floors. Ethnic celebrations,
exhibits and entertainment are often featured. Center House has an information booth on the main
floor, a cash machine, meeting rooms, police and
security, executive offices for Seattle Center and
the Seattle Symphony, and restrooms on all three
floors toward the back (north). There are also
restrooms on the grounds under the Flag Pavilion
and on the corner of the Northwest Court Buildings near the **KeyArena** (the former **Coliseum**).

Restaurant & shop hours:
11am-7pm or later; call for info.
Breakfast & coffee places open earlier.

THE CHILDREN'S MUSEUM

The recently expanded Children's Museum is
located on the lower level of Center House. It has
a two-story mountain for children to explore,
several homes from different countries, and hands-
on exhibits and activities; there is also a gift shop.

Hours: 10am-5pm daily.

Cost: $4.50 per person. Children
          under 12 months free.

Phone: 441-1768

The **Group Theatre** is adjacent to the Children's Museum on the lower level.

SEATTLE CHILDREN'S THEATRE

Located in the new **Charlotte Martin Theatre**
on Second Avenue North and Thomas Street, the
Seattle Children's Theatre features plays designed
for young audiences and families. Regular season
is September-June, with special productions in the

summer. The theater has expanded into space formerly occupied by the **Pacific Arts Center**.

Phone: 443-0807

THE FUN FOREST

The amusement park, known as the Fun Forest, covers the grounds between Center House and the Space Needle. Rides are divided into two sections: tame for younger and wild for older kids. There are also games, miniature golf, a video arcade, and refreshment and souvenir stands. Prices of rides and games vary.

Hours: Summer: daily, noon-midnight.
            Spring & fall: most weekends,
            depending upon the weather.

Phone: 684-7200,
            or 684-7165 (recording)

In the summer, concerts are held two or three times a week on the **Mural Amphitheatre** stage, where the audience can bask on the lawn while listening. The Venetian glass tile mosaic wall was designed by Paul Horiuchi for the World's Fair.

THE PACIFIC SCIENCE CENTER

The Pacific Science Center is a legacy of the World Fair's U.S. Science Pavilion. It has marvelous hands-on science exhibits for all ages, including life-like dinsaurs, game-playing robots and virtual reality, a **Planetarium**, the **Spacerium** for laser light shows, and the three-story **IMAX Theater**. The gift shop and the deli-type restaurant are open to the public without an admission fee. There are several restrooms in the buildings.

The Science Center is located on the Second Avenue side of Seattle Center; from the Space Needle or Center House, pass by the Mural Amphitheatre and look for the Science Center's graceful white arches designed by Minoru Yamisaki. The entrance on Denny Way is flanked by large topiary dinosaurs.

Hours: 10am-5pm weekdays;
            10am-6pm weekends.
            Summer: 10am-6pm daily.

Cost: Adults $6.50.
            Children 6-13 & seniors $5.50.
            (Seniors, free Wed.)
            Kids 2-5, $3.50.
            Prices are for admission to
            exhibits only; the Laserium and
            IMAX theaters have
            additional fees.

Phone: 443-2001 or 443-IMAX

The **Flag Pavilion** houses special functions and exhibits. The **Flag Plaza** in front of it is often the site of summer concerts and has an ice skating rink in the winter.

The former **Coliseum** has been remodelled and renamed the **Key Arena**. It is home for the Seattle SuperSonics basketball games and special events.

NORTHWEST CRAFT CENTER

The Northwest Craft Center shows and sells fine examples of Northwest pottery and other craft items. Established in 1963 after the fair, it is located in the low building on the north side of the Key Arena facing the International Fountain.

Hours: 11am-6pm Tues-Sun.
            Summer: 11am-6pm daily.

Cost: Free.

Phone: 728-1555

The **International Fountain**, the centerpiece of the grounds, has also been remodelled from its original World's Fair design. Its new mechanism retains its dancing water and music.

The buildings along Mercer Street (the **Bagley Wright Theatre, Playhouse**, and **Opera House**) house Seattle's performing arts: the symphony, ballet, opera, and theater companies. They are generally open only for performances. However, the Bagley Wright has public tours on Mondays, by appointment only (phone 443-2210). Exhibits and trade shows are held in the **Exhibition Hall**; the **Arena** is a multipurpose building used for ice hockey, trade shows, banquets, etc. On a nice day, a stroll around Seattle Center's 74-acre land-scaped grounds with its many small courtyards, fountains and works of art is delightful.

Getting to Seattle Center

In addition to the Monorail (page 32), several buses go to Seattle Center: #3, 4, 6, and 16 stop on the Space Needle side on Fifth Avenue; #1, 2, 13, 15, and 18 stop on First Avenue North by the Coli-seum. Call Metro, 553-3000, for information. Note: Seattle Center is outside the Ride Free Zone.

Or take the Waterfront Streetcar to its northern terminus at Broad Street and walk five blocks up Broad Street to Seattle Center.

Driving: Located on the north side of down-town, Seattle Center is accessible from Denny Way, Valley Street (referred to locally as "the Mercer Street mess," or First, Third or Fourth Avenues. There are many parking lots nearby (but not enough when there are major events on the grounds); prices vary. Valet parking is offered by the Space Needle for restaurant patrons.

In and Around

Some of Seattle's favorite places are a few minutes outside of the downtown area, easily accessible by Metro buses or a 15- to 20-minute drive. In addition to the listings in this section, many spots of special interest in the AND MORE section are close to downtown Seattle: see the Breweries, Gardens, Museums, Recreation, Shopping and Wineries chapters for more ideas.

Most destinations in this section can be visited quickly if time is short, but these spots invite leisurely strolls and picnic lunches on warm days.

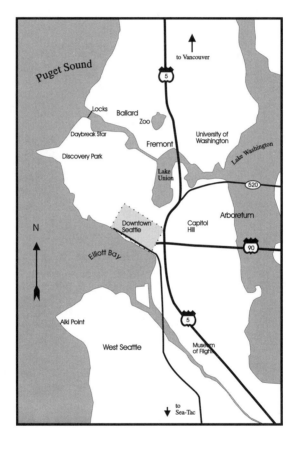

Greater Seattle

THE LOCKS

The **Hiram M. Chittenden Locks** — known variously as the **Chittenden Locks**, the **Government Locks**, the **Ballard Locks**, the **Salmon Ladder**, or simply the **Locks** — are located on the west end of the **Lake Washington Ship Canal**. Completed in 1917 after years of deliberations, they were named for the engineer who designed them. Originally envisioned as a way to open the areas to the east on the shores of Lake Washington for commercial purposes, the waterway is used by pleasure boaters and commercial vessels going between saltwater **Puget Sound** and freshwater **Lake Union** and **Lake Washington**. The present **Fish Ladder** was built in 1976 to facilitate the salmon migration back to freshwater spawning grounds.

Visiting the Locks is always popular, but it's especially nice to do on a sunny summer day. There's lots of activity as the lock operators direct boats' crews and the water raises or lowers the boats. Visitors may walk across the locks while the lock gates are closed.

The Fish Ladder with underwater windows for viewing salmon and trout is on the south side of the locks. The heaviest fish runs are in the summer months. In recent years, sea lions have been visible on the west side of the locks attracted by steelhead returning to spawn. The beautifully landscaped **Carl S. English, Jr. Botanical Garden** on the terraces of the north side and **Commodore Park** on the south are perfect for taking in the action or relaxing with a picnic lunch. On most weekends during the summer there are family activities or concerts.

The Visitor Center, located on the north side of the locks, has a narrated slide show and displays about the locks' history and construction. Restrooms are located on both the north and south sides. There are snack carts and restaurants near the entrance on the north side.

To learn more about the Locks, Garden and Fish Ladder, take the free guided walking tour.

Tours: June 1-Sept 30: daily at 1pm
         & 3:00pm.
         Oct 1-May 31: Sat & Sun at
         2pm, at the Visitor Center.

Hours: The park grounds open at 7am
         and close at 9pm. The Visitor
         Center is open daily 10am-7pm
         daily June thru Sept; and 11am-
         5pm Thurs- Mon., Oct thru
         May.
         The Locks and Fish Ladder are
         always open to boats and fish.

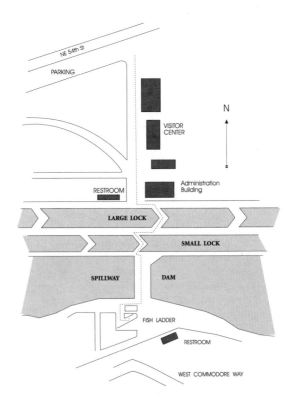

The Hiram M. Chittenden Locks

Cost:	Free.
Phone:	783-7059

Getting to the Locks:

3015 NW 54th Street

Driving: From downtown Seattle, take Westlake Avenue across the Fremont Bridge and bear
left onto Fremont Avenue at the second light from
the north end of the bridge. (Richard Beyer's popular sculpture **"Waiting for the Interurban"** is
on the right side at the north end of the Fremont
Bridge.) Continue bearing left on Leary Way into
Ballard and turn left onto Market Street. The
Locks are approximately a mile farther to the west
on the left side of the street.

Or, go north on Elliott Avenue across the Ballard Bridge to the Ballard exit just off the north
end of the bridge. Turn left onto Leary Way, go
under the bridge and continue on Leary, following
the signs to the Locks, to Market Street. Turn left
(west) onto Market Street in Ballard and continue
to the Locks on the left side of the road.

Either way, from downtown Seattle the drive
will take 15-20 minutes.

By bus: Take #17 from downtown. Call Metro,
553-3000, for information.

Gray Line's City Bus Tours stop on the south
side of the Locks. Call Gray Line, 626-5208.

FREMONT

Local residents have dubbed their community
"The Republic of Fremont" and take great pride in
their place in the world. Just north of the orange
and blue Fremont bridge, a pole in the middle of a
street divider proclaims its location to be the center of the universe, with distances marked to other
noteworthy locations. Drivers waiting for the
bridge to open gaze upon a neon Repunzel letting
down her hair on the northwest tower. To the east,
the Fremont Troll grips a Volkswagon under the
freeway on 36th Street. On summer weekends
locals bring couches to watch movies in a parking
lot transformed into an outdoor theater.

DAYBREAK STAR CENTER

Daybreak Star Indian Cultural Center, on the edge of **Discovery Park**, is operated by the United Indians of All Tribes Foundation. The Center displays Native American art from the four geographic tribal regions throughout the building. There are several large carved wood pieces, the Sacred Circle Gallery of American Indian Art that shows works by contemporary artists, and a gift shop with attractive items, books and cards. The Center also has community center facilities, including meeting rooms, day care, and outdoor playground equipment. Tours are available by appointment.

Hours:	10am-5pm, Mon.-Sat; noon-5pm, Sun.
Phone:	285-4425

The grounds have more works of art, including one of the large terra-cotta Indian heads saved from the White-Henry-Stuart building when it was demolished to make way for the Rainier Tower. The view looking north to **Shilshole Marina** and up Puget Sound to Whidbey Island and beyond is one of the most spectacular in Seattle.

The annual **Seafair Indian Days Pow-Wow** the end of July attracts Native Americans from the U.S. and Canada for a festive weekend of dancing, singing and drumming.

Discovery Park, the former site of Fort Lawton, has been left in a natural state with trails wandering down the hillside to West Point.

Getting to Daybreak Star:

Daybreak Star is located on the north side of Discovery Park, about 20 minutes from downown.

By car: Follow Commodore Way from the south side of the Locks heading west into Discovery Park and take the first right turn.

By bus: #33 from downtown Seattle goes to Discovery Park and Daybreak Star Cultural Center. Call Metro, 553-3000, for information.

FISHERMEN'S TERMINAL

Fishermen's Terminal at **Salmon Bay** is home to one of the world's largest fleet of salmon and halibut trollers. Built in 1914 when the locks were constructed, the facilities were redeveloped recently, with buildings and docks enlarged to accommodate modern fishing boats and processors.

Signs of the fishing industry abound: Nets dry on the pavement and in the oversized sheds at the east side of the complex, boats of all types line the wharves, and marine hardware supplies are available at several chandleries. Fish engravings on the glass bricks in the Terminal Center building represent local species. The walls of Chinook's restaurant are covered with pictures of local boats and crews, and the Terminal's restaurants and bars cater to fishermen and visitors.

Take in the scene from the benches near the **Seattle Fishermen's Memorial statue**, engraved with names of local fishermen lost at sea.

The shops in the Terminal stock gear and supplies for the fishing industry. Captain's has navigation charts, an extensive collection of books about boats and fishing, and some nautical gifts. The Wild Salmon fish market sells the daily catch. There is also a pipe and tobacco shop. Public restrooms and telephones are near the Bay Cafe.

For information, phone 728-3395.

Getting to Fishermen's Terminal:

From downtown Seattle, head north on Elliott Avenue, bearing right as it becomes 15th Avenue West. Continue heading north to the Emerson Street exit. Watch for signs for Port of Seattle Fishermen's Terminal, south of the Ballard Bridge, about a 10-minute drive from downtown.

By bus: Take #15 or #18 from downtown Seattle; get off at Emerson Street, before the Ballard Bridge and go down the stairs to Emerson, then walk west about four blocks. Call Metro, 553-3000, for information.

WOODLAND PARK ZOO

Seattle's Woodland Park Zoo has won recognition and awards in recent years for its open exhibits where animals wander in their natural habitats. Elephants walk, and occasionally work, in the spacious Elephant Forest. Nearby animals roam the African Savanna; a knoll with a brass plaque in memory of Seattle-born rock star **Jimi Hendrix** has a view of the area. The zoo's newest exhibit, Trail of Vines, is a lush tropical forest adjacent to the Elephant Forest. The Tropical Rain Forest and The Nocturnal House have many rare plants and animals under their roofs. Displays with informative signs blend into the beautifully landscaped grounds.

A Family Farm area and Petting Zoo have typical farm animals and, depending on the season, their babies. The Northern Trail exhibit, home of Northwest animals and bald eagles, surrounds the Conservation Yards. At the Raptor Center, injured or sick eagles and other raptors are nursed back to health before being released. Elephant baths and other activities are scheduled daily, and special programs are held throughout the year. Summer concerts raise money for zoo programs.

The Rain Forest Cafe by the West Entrance has several mini restaurants under its roof and is open throughout the year. Or bring your own picnic and use the large grassy area on the north side of the grounds. There are several restrooms on the grounds

Strollers and wheelchairs may be rented, depending upon availability, at the Zoo Store inside the South Entrance.

Hours:	Daily, 8:30am-6pm Apr-Sept; 8:30am-5pm March & Oct; 9:30am-4pm Nov-Feb. Note: Some exhibits close early.
Cost:	Adults $7.50. Seniors $5.75. Youths 6-17 & disabled $5. Children 3-5, $2.75.

Reduced prices Nov-Feb and
for King County residents.

Phone: 684-4800

Getting to Woodland Park Zoo:

Driving: From downtown Seattle, take I-5
heading north to exit 169, NE 50th Street, and
head west, following the signs for the Zoo. There
are also signs from the 45th Street exit from I-5.

Or, from Hwy 99, head north and exit at 45th
Avenue. Turn left at the stop sign onto 45th Ave-
nue and head west, staying in the right-hand lane,
to Fremont Avenue. Turn right onto Fremont
Avenue and go north to 50th Avenue to the South
Entrance of the Zoo.

There are pay parking lots near the entrances
on 50th and Fremont Avenue, the West Entrance
on Phinney Avenue, and the North Entrance on
59th Street; parking costs $3.50. The Zoo is about
15 minutes from downtown.

By bus: Take #5 from downtown Seattle
directly to the West Entrance. Call Metro,
553-3000, for information.

THE ROSE GARDEN
AT WOODLAND PARK

Grass pathways circulate through the $2\frac{1}{2}$-acre
formal Rose Garden on the south side of the Zoo.
The garden's extensive collection of all types of
roses is open the same hours as the Zoo.

Cost: Free.

Phone: 684-4863

The Zoo occupies the west half of **Woodland
Park**; **Green Lake** is to the north. Seattle's most
popular park, Green Lake, has playfields, tennis
courts and a miniature golf course. Joggers, skaters and walkers vie for space on the three-mile
path around the lake, while in the lake, eight-
oared shells and sail boarders share the water with
intrepid ducks and geese.

THE UNIVERSITY OF WASHINGTON

The University of Washington, the premier school in the state university system, is a few minutes north of downtown, just east of the I-5 freeway. Theaters, museums, libraries, athletic facilities and classroom buildings for the university's 35,000 students are located throughout the spacious grounds.

The **Olmsted Brothers** firm, planners of New York's Central Park and Seattle's extensive park system, designed the campus for Seattle's 1909 **Alaskan-Yukon Pacific Exposition** (known as the AYP. The **Drumheller Fountain** in the middle of **Frosh Pond** and the breathtaking view of Mt. Rainier continue to be the campus's centerpieces. There are many gardens and groves throughout the grounds; one of the most interesting is the **Medicinal Herb** (or **Drug Plant**) **Garden** across from the Forestry buildings.

The university's two major museums are open to the public. At the north end of the campus, marked by totem poles, the **Burke Museum** (phone 543-5590) has permanent early Northwest Native American and natural history exhibits featuring local dinosaurs and Indian artifacts, a traditional cedar plank house, and a Discovery Room for hands-on explorations. Special shows change about every two months. A side room on the main floor dedicated to the Burke family has stunning Tiffany glass windows. The coffee shop downstairs, known as the Boiserie, is in an elegant room with paneling from an 18th-century European chateau. The Universty's art museum, **The Henry Art Gallery** (phone 543-2280) on 15th Avenue is undergoing major expansion and renovation. It will reopen in spring of 1997.

The school has spread beyond the original grounds to include buildings scattered throughout the 700-acre campus. **Husky Stadium** and **Hec Edmundson Pavilion**, where the UW's Husky teams play, are on the campus's east side along

Montlake Boulevard. An unusual man-made climbing rock is in the parking lot near the Water Activities Building. The medical complex is on NE Pacific Street along the Montlake Cut (or Canal).

The Visitor Information Center, 4014 University Way NE, has general University area information and brochures. For a self-guided tour of the campus pick up a Campus Walk Map, which has historical information about campus buildings and sights in addition to its walking tour.

Hours: 8am-5pm weekdays.

Phone: 543-9198

Campus maps and information are also available at **Schmitz Hall**, Room 320, at 15th Avenue and Campus Parkway, and at the booths at campus entrances. To drive through the campus, ask for a free 15-minute pass at an entrance booth. Parking is available in campus lots.

Free guided campus tours for prospective students lasting approximately $1\frac{1}{2}$ hours are given 2:30pm weekdays, departing from Schmitz Hall, Room 320. Phone 543-9686 for information.

Getting to the University:

By car: Take I-5 heading north to the 45th Street exit. Head east on 45th Street, following the signs, to the northern campus entrance on the right at 17th Avenue. The campus is about 15 minutes from downtown Seattle.

By bus: Several buses, 70, 71, 72, 73, 74, and 83, go to the University area. Because the campus is so large, call Metro, 553-3000, for information about getting to a specific area.

THE ARBORETUM

The 200-acre **Washington Park Arboretum**, between Madison Street and Lake Washington, is part of Seattle's extensive park system designed by the **Olmsted Brothers** firm of Brookline, Mass. Plantings with informative signs are grouped throughout the grounds by species. The rhododendrons, Washington's state flower, and azaleas are spectacular in spring when they are in bloom. One of the largest public gardens in the U.S., the Arboretum is renowned for its Japanese Maples, hollies, firs, camellias, magnolias and maples. Referred to as a "living museum," it's a great place to visit on foot or bicycle for a picnic lunch. In the summer swimmers and canoeists enjoy the water around **Foster Island** on the north side of the park. A half-mile trail through Foster Island begins at the **Museum of History and Industry** and is accessible from the land north of the Arboretum.

Heavily traveled Lake Washington Boulevard meanders through the Arboretum from Madison Street to the University; Arboretum Drive East, the high road to the east, is more scenic and slower paced. The Arboretum and Arboretum Drive East close at sunset but the main roads remain open all the time.

Hours:	Open daily dawn to dusk.
Cost:	Free.
Phone:	543-8800

THE VISITOR INFORMATION CENTER

The Graham Visitor Information Center is located in the northeast section, on Arboretum Drive East. Volunteers sell trail maps, books, plant accessories, and a small selection of plants. Restrooms are located in the building.

Hours:	10am-4pm weekdays; 12noon-4pm weekends.

| Tours: | Free guided walking tours depart from the Visitor Information Center Sundays at 1pm. |

JAPANESE GARDEN

An authentic Japanese Garden covering $3\frac{1}{2}$ acres is located in the southwest corner of the Arboretum grounds. The garden, described as "a compressed world of mountains, forest, lakes, rivers, tablelands, and a village, each with a quiet message of its own," is set off from the rest of the Arboretum. A **Japanese Tea Service** is performed the third Sunday of the month. Note: The gravel pathways may be difficult to negotiate with wheelchairs and strollers.

Hours:	10am-6pm daily; later in spring and summer. Closed Dec-Feb.
Cost:	Adults $2.50. 19 & under and seniors, $1.50. Under 6 free.
Phone:	684-4725.

Getting to the Arboretum:

By car: To the Arboretum's north end: From downtown Seattle, take I-5 heading north. Take exit #168B (Bellevue-Kirkland) to Hwy 520. Stay in the right lane and take the first exit, approximately one mile (Montlake/University of Washington). Stay in the right lane of the exit ramp and go straight through the intersection; the road becomes Lake Washington Boulevard. Bear left after approximately half a mile when the road forks at 24th Avenue. At the stop sign in the middle of the intersection, go left to the Information Center and Arboretum Drive East (the sign says "Office & Greenhouse") or right along Lake Washington Boulevard.

Or, to the south side: Drive east on Madison Avenue to Lake Washington Boulevard; the entrance to the Arboretum is on the left. Driving time either way is 10 to 15 minutes.

By bus: Take #11 to the southern Arboretum entrance at the intersection of Madison Avenue and Lake Washington Boulevard. The Japanese Garden is about ¼ mile to the north; the Visitor Center approximately one mile.

Or take #43 or #25 and get off at 24th Avenue and East Lynn. The Visitor Center is approximately ¼ mile to the east.

The Washington Park Arboretum

MUSEUM OF FLIGHT

The Museum of Flight has two outstanding galleries filled with facts and flying machines. Visits start with vintage planes — the first Air Force One, a Sabre F-86, and a Grumman A-6E — on the grounds outside the museum. An imposing Flight Control Tower looks out over the runway so visitors see and hear air traffic on a working runway from a controller's perspective. Inside, in the restored **Red Barn** where Boeing built its first planes, there are informative exhibits depicting the history of flight.

Dozens of planes hang from the ceiling and are displayed on the floor of the elegant glass-walled Great Gallery. A sleek, menacing Blackbird with its drone and a World War II Corsair are on the floor, while to the side, the Apollo command module is the center of an exhibit about manned space exploration. Other famous planes include the Gossamer Albatross II, the back-up to the plane that made the first human-powered flight, and a B-29. The view from the mezzanine balcony is superb. Kids — and adults — can climb into planes and work their controls in the Hangar area.

Museum docents are available for short introductory tours, more extensive tours, or just to answer visitors' questions. Films about flight and aviation are shown daily in the theater, and special programs and films are scheduled throughout the year. A gift shop is located off the entry lobby and a restaurant is down the hall on the north end of the building. The museum hosts special events throughout the year including FlyerWorks!, which will be part of the Ivar's 4th of July festivities on Seattle's waterfront.

The museum is located on the west side of **Boeing Field**, also known as the **King County Airport**, about 15 minutes from downtown Seattle.

Hours: Daily,10am-5pm;
           Thurs, 10am-9pm.

Cost: Adults $6.
               Youths 6-15, $3.
               Under 6 free.
               Free the first Thurs of the
               month.

Phone: 764-5720

Getting to the Museum of Flight:

9404 E. Marginal Way South

Driving: From downtown Seattle, take I-5 heading south to exit 158 at the south end of Boeing Field. Head west for half a mile, then turn right onto East Marginal Way South and head north. The parking entrance is on the south side of the Red Barn.

Or take Hwy 99 heading south, keeping to the left when the road forks at the First Avenue South bridge; the road becomes East Marginal Way South. The entrance to the museum is on the left, just after the Red Barn. Either way, driving time is 15 to 20 minutes.

By bus: #174. Call Metro, 553-3000, for information.

Gray Line's Gold 'N' Wings tour stops at the Museum of Flight (phone626-5208).

Out and About

While Seattle is the heart of Puget Sound, the outlying areas share the city's soul. Nearby towns have their own history and personalities and fill out the fabric of the Northwest. Trips to Victoria, the Olympic Peninsula or Mount Rainier offer a complete change of pace from the city. The shorter trips in this section — Boeing and Snoqualmie Falls — can be done in a half day, but often are enhanced with side trips. The longer trips could be done in one day, if only by a cursory visit. However, it seems a shame to try to see everything quickly and end up exhausted when an overnight trip would be much more enjoyable.

The trips in this section assume the visitor will be driving, but where public transportation is available it is listed.

BOEING TOUR CENTER, EVERETT

Boeing's Everett facility is where more than 20,000 of Boeing's 80,000 Seattle area employees produce its wide-body planes, the 747 and 767, and the new 777s.

The 90-minute tours of the facility begin with an informative movie extolling Boeing's accomplishments. Buses then take visitors to the largest (by volume) building in the world to see and hear the production lines, followed by a drive around the grounds to view the finished products. The tour guides are knowledgeable and full of superlatives: the biggest, the most, the first, etc.

The shop area is cool inside and because of the building's size it is a long walk. It is wheelchair accessible. **Children under 4 feet, 2 inches tall and still and video cameras are not permitted.** The Tour Center has historical photographs, a small gift shop and restrooms. Tours fill up quickly in the summer; it's best to go early.

Hours:	9, 10, 11am; 1, 2, & 3pm. Tours are weekdays only, no holidays, on a first-come, first-served basis.
Cost:	Free.
Phone:	1-800-464-1476

Getting to the Boeing Tour Center:

Driving: Go north on I-5 or on I-405 to I-5 exit 189 (approximately a half-hour from Seattle). Head west (the left lane of the exit ramp) on SR 526 for three miles and follow the signs for Boeing Tour Center. Driving time from Seattle is 30-40 minutes.

It is possible to get there by public transportation, but not easy — transportation time each way is approximately two hours. Phone 1-800-562-1375 for **Community Transit information**.

Gray Line offers Boeing tours departing from

downtown Seattle at 2pm or 2:30pm; days and
times vary depending on the time of year.

Cost: $32.50.

Phone: 626-5208

The **Mosquito Fleet** has tours of the Boeing
plant departing from Everett's hotels or Marina
Village. The 4-hour tour includes an historical
tour of the city.

Cost: Adults $25. Seniors $22.50.
               17 & under $20.

Phone: 206-252-6800

SNOHOMISH

Snohomish, a thriving lumber town at the turn
of the century, is now known for its numerous antique shops. Most are located on the main street or
in the Antique Mall at the end of town. One block
east an original Carnegie Library building is still
in use. Many fine Victorian homes in the nearby
residential area remain from the early days. The
town is located a few miles east of Everett on
Rte 2.

EDMONDS

The small, attractive town of Edmonds is half-
way between Seattle and Everett, on the water
west of I-5. The waterfront south of the ferry
terminal is full of marinas and restaurants with
terrific views of Puget Sound and the Kitsap Peninsula. Streets are lined with flowers, small shops,
galleries and restaurants. A log cabin housing the
Chamber of Commerce office (phone 1-206-776-
6711) is next door to the **Historical Museum** on
Fifth Avenue North, just off Main Street.

Getting to Edmonds:

Look for the Edmonds/Kingston Ferry signs on
I-5 and follow the road into town. To get to downtown Edmonds avoid the right-hand shoulder
ferry-traffic lane as you approach downtown.

SNOQUALMIE FALLS

Spectacular Snoqualmie Falls, located just outside of the small town of Snoqualmie, is an easy 45-minute drive from Seattle. A popular place to visit during summer months, the 268-foot falls are most impressive after heavy rains or during spring run-offs. An observation deck and covered picnic tables are nearby, as well as a snack bar, souvenir shop and restrooms. A trail from the top leads down to the old Puget Power plant at the base of the falls.

The **Salish Lodge** overlooking the falls has a lounge upstairs, a country clothing shop and a restaurant featuring gourmet meals; call ahead for reservations: 1-206-888-2556.

On weekends during the summer and holidays the **Puget Sound & Snoqualmie Valley Railroad** steam train runs between **North Bend** and the west side of Snoqualmie Falls, with a stop in Snoqualmie. Call 1-206-888-2206 for information (see Trains, page 124.)

The historic train depot in Snoqualmie houses a small museum full of logging items from the area; the former waiting room has been turned into a bookstore (open on weekends when the steam train operates). Look for the enormous log, typical of the area's original old-growth trees, and the bandsaw used to cut them, on the green.

Television's "**Twin Peaks**" fans still come to Snoqualmie and North Bend to savor cherry pie and have a "damn fine cup of joe."

Getting to Snoqualmie Falls:

From I-90 heading east, take the Snoqualmie exit, #27. Turn left, under the freeway, and follow the signs to Snoqualmie and Snoqualmie Falls. Turn left after $\frac{1}{4}$ mile; go approximately $\frac{3}{4}$ mile then left again at the stop sign, and the falls are about a mile away. The road is well-marked. Driving time from Seattle is approximately 45 minutes.

There are several places along I-90 to stop en route to the falls: In Issaquah, **Gilman Village**, exit 15, has restaurants, bakeries and shops (see Shopping, page 113). **Boehm's Chocolates**, just east of exit 17 (Front Street) on Gilman Boulevard, makes its rich European-style chocolates on the premises. Exhibits in the **Cougar Mountain Zoological Park** (phone 206-391-5508) focus on endangered species. On clear days Mt. Rainier is visible behind the **Issaquah Alps**.

The **Herbfarm**, a ten-minute drive from the Preston/Fall City exit, #22, has landscaped herb gardens, plants for sale, a gift shop and a restaurant (phone 206-784-2222). Spring and summer are the best times to see its full array of plantings, the llamas and other animals.

A few miles farther east at exit 27, just off the Snoqualmie Falls exit, the **Snoqualmie Winery** sits on a hillside with a spectacular view of the Snoqualmie Valley, Mt. Si, and the Cascades. (See Wineries, page 130). The **Snoqualmie Valley Historical Museum** in nearby North Bend has articles and photographs depicting life in the area from its earliest settlements. Phone 206-888-3200 for information.

Buses 210, 211, and 213 serve this area from Seattle. Call Metro, 553-3000, for information.

Snoqualmie Falls

TACOMA

Downtown Tacoma is a reminder of the city's boom and bust history — fine old buildings stand neglected next to empty lots or nondescript newer structures. But recently several of its most elegant heirlooms have been rehabilitated and are glowing with new life. The ornate Union Station on Pacific Avenue has become a new Federal Building, full of huge glass pieces, while a few blocks away in the theater district, the grand Pantages and Rialto theaters are once again alive with performances, joined by the new Theatre on the Square.

Museums and art galleries abound: **The Washington State Historical Society Museum** located in its new building at 1911 Pacific Avenue (phone 206-593-2830) and the **Tacoma Art Museum** (phone 206-272-4383) feature area history and artists. Two self-guided tour maps of historic buildings are available.

Tacoma's view parks show off its spectacular location: Mt. Rainier gleams to the east on clear days, while Puget Sound embraces the city on the west. **Point Defiance Park** has a scenic Five-Mile Drive through beaches, old-growth woods, and views of islands and the Olympic Mountains. The **Point Defiance Zoo and Aquarium** is located in the park, with hilly paths leading to exhibits featuring Northwest animals (phone 206-591-5337). **Fort Nisqually** is a reproduction of the original fort built by fur traders (phone 206-591-5339).

For information about the area call Tacoma Visitors' Information, 800-272-2662. Getting there: Drive south on I-5, about 45 minutes. The large blue dome on the right is the **Tacoma Dome**, used for sports and concerts.

GIG HARBOR

Across the **Tacoma Narrows Bridge** is the picturesque town of Gig Harbor. The fishing industry still thrives here among the gift shops, galleries and restaurants. The view-filled walk around the U-shaped harbor to the City Park across the bay is about two miles.

MOUNT RAINIER

At 14,411 feet (4,392 meters), majestic Mount Rainier is the fifth highest mountain in the United States and the highest of the volcanic peaks in Washington.

The native Indians called it Tahoma, meaning "white mountain" and believed it was inhabited by spirits. In 1792 when Captain George Vancouver explored the Puget Sound region, he named the mountain in honor of Peter Rainier, a fellow English sea captain who never saw it.

Mt. Rainier, known locally as "the mountain," can be seen from spots throughout the Puget Sound area (see Views, page 124). It is breathtaking up close. En route the road passes through majestic forests as it climbs to the visitors' centers. On the mountain, Rainier's size and grandeur are overwhelming. Trails with spectacular views wander through meadows of flowers studded with wind-bent trees. Most years there is snow by the parking lots or along the trails throughout the summer.

The highest elevation in Mt. Rainier National Park accessible by automobile is 6,400 feet at **Sunrise**. The Sunrise Visitor Information Center has food service, campers' supplies and a gift shop. The road to Sunrise branches off from the White River entrance and is not open in the winter.

The facilities at **Paradise**, altitude 5,400 feet, are more extensive. The large, round Visitors Center has displays and movies about the park. Park Service personnel are available to answer questions and also lead trail walks, identifying flora and fauna along the way. A snack bar and gift shop are located in the Visitors Center and in the grand old **Paradise Inn** a little farther up the road. The Paradise Inn also has hotel facilities and a dining room, renowned for its Sunday brunch. **Note:** in winter the Paradise Inn is closed and the Visitors Center is open only on weekends; however, bathroom facilities in the Visitors Center are always open.

Trails in Rainier's subalpine area, marked with

appproximate walking times, start from the parking lot. Pets must be kept on leash in the park and are not allowed on trails.

Park admission is $5 a car. There are no gas stations in the park. See page 63 for phone numbers and resources for Mt. Rainier information.

Getting to Mount Rainier:

There are two routes from Seattle to Mount Rainier, both with spectacular views and attractions along the way. Driving time from Seattle is approximately $2\frac{1}{2}$ hours each way not including stops. Most people do the trip in one day, going to the park one way and returning the other, to see as much as possible. Pullout spots along the road indicate that there's something extraordinary to see —it's tempting to stop at every one. The side roads in the towns along the way often have fine old buildings and homes, built when the area prospered from coal, lumber or agriculture. Note: There was extensive damage from the 1996 winter rains and some roads and trails may be closed.

Through **Maple Valley** and **Enumclaw:**
(Note: this entrance to Mount Rainier is closed in the winter.)

Head east on I-90, then south on I-405 to exit #4, marked Renton/Enumclaw SR 169, south of I-90. This exit from I-405 is tricky; watch for the signs to Enumclaw. Follow the road through **Maple Valley** to **Black Diamond**, a former coal mining area known now for its brick-oven bakery a few blocks west of the highway. Just south of Black Diamond the road crosses over the spectacular **Green River Gorge**. The road between Black Diamond and **Enumclaw** goes through rolling farm lands and pastures at the base of the foothills with stunning views of Mt. Rainier. From Enumclaw it is approximately 40 miles through the forest to the Mt. Rainier White River entrance on SR 410. The Forest Service Information Centers, on the right side of the road past Greenwater and another at the park entrance, have maps and information about the area. The road to **Crystal Moun-**

tain, the state's largest ski area, is on the left, outside the log gateway marking the park entrance. The Crystal Mountain road is open year- round. Crystal also has summer tourist facilities.

Through **Puyallup** and **Longmire:**

The road from Longmire to Paradise is open year-round, but driving restrictions may apply in the winter (November-May). For highway information call: 1-206-569-2211.

Head south on I-5 to exit 142A to Puyallup and Mt. Rainier. Follow the signs for Puyallup (home of the **Western Washington State Fair**); there isn't much warning before exits or turns. Then follow SR 161 to Eatonville, Rte 7 to Elbe, then Rte 706 to Ashford. Longmire is about five miles inside the park entrance, 85 miles southeast of Seattle. There are no gas stations inside the park. Note: returning to Seattle, highway signs are sparse; stay on the main road through Puyallup until you come to signs for I-5.

NORTHWEST TREK WILDLIFE PARK

Northwest Trek, about a half-hour south of Puyallup on SR 161, is a 635-acre wildlife park with guided tram tours of indigenous Northwest animals roaming free in their natural habitats. The grounds have educational wildlife exhibits, nature trails, and a restaurant.

Hours:	Summer: 9:30am-6pm daily. Winter: Fri.-Sun. & holidays, 9:30am-3pm. Call for schedule. Tours on the hour.
Cost:	Adults $7.85. Seniors $7.00. Youths 5-17, $5.50; 3-4, $3.50. Under 3, free.
Phone:	1-360-832-6116; 1-800-433-TREK

The vintage **steam train** in the small town of **Elbe** runs on weekends during the summer (see

Trains, page 124). For information, phone the **Mt. Rainier Scenic Railroad**, 360-569-2588. The tiny church in Elbe, which holds 27 people, is a national historical monument and is open to the public.

There are several restaurants along the way featuring homemade breads, soups and pies; many have wonderful wild blackberry treats.

The old **National Park Inn** at Longmire, also known as the **Longmire Inn**, is open year-round, 8am-5pm. Recently remodeled, it has rooms, food service, souvenirs, and some groceries (phone 360-569-2412). The **Longmire Museum** next door is one of the original Park Service Museums with exhibits describing the geology and wildlife of the park. In winter, cross-country ski equipment and information are available at the **Ski Touring Center** to the right of the Inn; phone 360-569-2412 for information.

In summer there's whitewater rafting, horseback riding and bicycling in the area. Hours and days of operation change in winter and many places are closed; call to confirm before making plans.

Gray Line offers day and overnight bus tours to Mt. Rainier from May through October. Phone: 626-5208. **Scenic Bound Tours Co.** has one-day van tours to Mt. Rainier or **Mount St. Helens**, call 443-6907.

For information about Mount Rainier:

National Park Service, Henry M. Jackson Federal Building, 2nd Avenue, between Madison and Marion, Seattle, 98101. Phone: 220-7450.

National Park Service, Tahoma Woods, Star Route, Ashford, WA, 98304. Phone: 1-360-569-2211.

Mt. Rainier Guest Services, P.O. Box 108, Ashford, WA, 98304. Phone: 1-360-569-2275.

Twenty-four hour recorded highway and general information:1-360-569-2211.

THE OLYMPIC PENINSULA

The small towns and broad vistas of the Olympic Peninsula are packed with Northwest history — reminders of America's past. Known for its natural beauty, the area has many different climates: The rain forest receives as much as 200 inches of rain a year, while to the east, in the rainshadow of the Olympic mountains, Sequim receives less than 20.

A one-day trip doesn't allow enough time to enjoy the area; an overnight stay on the Peninsula

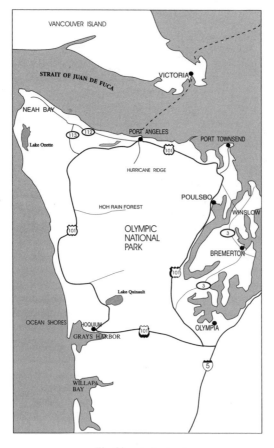

The Olympic Peninsula

would be better, especially for more distant destinations. Wander down back roads to see the area's charm and unspoiled beauty.

The **Seattle-Bainbridge Island ships** making the crossing between Seattle and Bainbridge are the largest and newest of the state ferry system. The ride takes half an hour and on a clear day the views are spectacular. Foot passengers can easily visit the town of **Winslow**, a short walk from the ferry dock, to sightsee or have a meal before returning to Seattle. The **Bainbridge Island Winery** is also within walking distance of the ferry terminal: continue straight ahead on Hwy 305 for ¼ mile. It's open afternoons, Wednesday-Sunday.

Driving north from Winslow on the **Kitsap Peninsula**, to either Port Townsend or Port Angeles takes about two hours, but may be longer depending upon traffic on the two-lane highway. The grave of **Chief Sealth**, the Indian chief who befriended Seattle's pioneer settlers, is in Suquamish, a short distance from the highway. The **Suquamish Indian Museum**, about 15 minutes by car from the ferry dock, is on the left just west of the Agate Pass Bridge; turn left at the traffic light. This small, attractive museum has pictorial exhibits, artifacts and a movie depicting Indian life in the area; open 11am-4pm daily. The town and the museum have nice beaches for picnics.

Driving northwest on Rte 305, you come next to the town of **Poulsbo**. To drive into town, turn left at the first traffic light onto Hostmark Street. The area's Scandinavian heritage is evident along the waterfront park and in the shops along Front Street. On the far side of town, the **Thomas Kemper Brewery** and Pub is open for tastes of their ales and root beers (phone 360-697-1446).

Continuing north, the road forks. To the east is **Port Gamble**, a former mill town complete with a country store and museum, but no restaurants. The ferry to **Edmonds** sails from **Kingston**, eight miles southeast of Port Gamble.

Or, to the west, the highway crosses the Hood Canal to the Olympic Peninsula on the **Hood**

Canal Floating Bridge, which sank during a wild winter storm in 1979. This bridge closes to vehicles during big storms; phone 1-360-437-2288 for bridge information. Beyond the bridge, the road to **Port Ludlow** branches off to the right. The resort has a golf course, hotel, and marine facilities.

Several roads lead to the picturesque town of **Port Townsend**, which has many charming 19th-century Victorian buildings, many now bed and breakfast inns, restaurants, and shops. Photographs and articles from the times when Port Townsend was vying to become the premier city in the Northwest are on display in the **Jefferson County Historical Museum** in City Hall on Water Street. The upper town on the hill where the gentry lived has a great country store, a movie theater and panoramic views of Puget Sound. General information and maps for self-guided city tours are available at the Chamber of Commerce office on Sims Way and the Visitor Information Center south of the ferry dock. The Port Townsend-Keystone ferry dock is on the main street at the south end of town, about a 10-minute walk or free bus ride from downtown. See Ferries, pages 99-102. Historic **Fort Worden**, where the movie "Officer and a Gentleman" was filmed, is to the north.

Continuing on Hwy 101 past the **Neuharth Winery**, the next town to the northwest is **Sequim**, a town popular with retirees because of its mild climate and scant 15-inch annual rainfall. Off the highway, the Sequim-Dungeness Road, marked by signs to the 3 Crabs Restaurant, has views of **Dungeness Spit**. The lighthouse at the tip of Dungeness Spit is open year-round; the walk out and back will take about two hours. The road continues past farms and pastures to the **Olympic Game Farm**, (phone 1-800-778-4295).

Back on Hwy 101, the last large town on the north end of the Peninsula is **Port Angeles**. The ferry dock for the **Black Ball Ferry** to Victoria is downtown near the Visitor Information Center. While waiting for the ferry, visit the Marine Labo-

ratory or the observation tower, or walk out on
Ediz Spit or along the waterfront trail. Off Hwy
101, the 18-mile trip to **Hurricane Ridge**, elevation 5,200 feet, offers spectacular views of Puget
Sound and the Strait of Juan de Fuca, and maybe
a view of **Mt. Olympus** on a clear day. A fee of
$5 per car is charged in the summer to enter
Olympic National Park and the other parks on
the Peninsula.

Hwy 112 splits off from Hwy 101 a few miles
west of Port Angeles and stays close to the coast.
The small towns along Hwy 112 have supplies for
the many people who come for the area's fishing.

Hwy 101 continues to the southwest around
Lake Crescent, which has lodging facilities,
many hiking trails and a paddlewheel boat (phone
360-452-4520) for tours of the lake. The road follows the west side of Olympic National Park,
passing through towns and Indian reservations
where logging and fishing are the main industries.

There are few roads in the area but the hiking
trails and campgrounds offer opportunities to see
the area's natural wilderness. This part of Hwy
101 is on the wet west side of the **Rain Forest**
where rainfall averages more than 150 inches a
year. On the coast, **Kalaloch Lodge** has cabins
and a dining room overlooking the ocean with
paths to sandy beaches and tide pools. Thirty
miles inland to the south, **Lake Quinault Lodge**
is surrounded by enormous old-growth trees. A
U.S. Forest Service Information office has information about trails and campgrounds throughout
the area.

Travelers can continue south to the beaches of
Ocean Shores or turn east at **Hoquium** and either
return to I-5 or head north on Hwy 101 and go
northwest on Rte 3 to Bremerton, where the **U.S.
Navy shipyards** are. The shipyards are not open
to the public, but for a good view of the moth-
balled fleet in the harbor, take a harbor tour from
Kitsap Harbor Tours (phone 360-377-8924), or
ride the passenger-only ferry to **Port Orchard**
(see Ferries, page 101). **Port Orchard's** many

galleries and antique shops make good browsing. The **Naval Museum**, loaded with history, is on **Bremerton**'s redeveloped waterfront area, up the street from the ferry dock. Docked nearby is the destroyer *USS Turner Joy*, which is open to the public (phone 360-792-2457).

Farther north on the **Kitsap Peninsula** is Keyport's free **Naval Museum of Underwater Technology**. This unique museum has weapons and vehicles used in underwater warfare and explorations; closed Tuesdays (phone 1-360-396-4148).

Returning to Seattle, the ferry from Bremerton wends its way through scenic waterways during the one-hour trip across Puget Sound.

Van tours of the area are available from **WeatherVane Tours** (phone 206-660-8687).

Information about the Olympic and Kitsap Peninsulas is available from local chambers of commerce and area information centers on the Olympic and Kitsap Peninsulas:

The **Bainbridge Island Chamber of Commerce**, 153 Madrone Lane, Winslow, WA 98110. Phone 360-842-3700.

The **Bremerton/Kitsap County Visitor & Convention Bureau**, 120 Washington Street, Bremerton, WA 98310. Phone 360-479-3588.

The **Kitsap Peninsula Visitor & Convention Bureau**, PO Box 1790, Silverdale, WA 98383. Phone 360-698-7411 or 1-800-416-5615.

The **Port Townsend Chamber of Commerce**, 2437 Sims Way, Port Townsend, WA 98368. Phone 360-385-2722.

The **Port Angeles Visitor Center**, 121 East Railroad Avenue, Port Angeles, WA 98362. Phone 360-452-2363.

VICTORIA

Victoria, the quaint town on the south side of Canada's **Vancouver Island**, is known for its flourishing gardens and English ambiance. Turn-of-the-century buildings on narrow roads house pubs, shops, inns and tea houses.

Two grand buildings face the inner harbor: the **Empress Hotel**, famed for its afternoon tea, and the **Parliament Building**, which is outlined with lights at night. Free guided tours of the Parliament Building are given most days, although some parts may be closed depending on the legislative calendar. Between the two is the large **Royal British Columbia Museum of Natural History** with four floors of exhibits about the Pacific Northwest; open daily. Around the Inner Harbour there are shops and tourist attractions.

The area's mild climate encourages abundant flowers and gardens. The grandest, **Butchart Gardens** (phone 604-652-4422), a few miles out of town, were built in a former limestone quarry and now are practically an institution — thousands come to see the imaginative plantings and evening fireworks shows.

For travelers going only to Victoria and not planning any further travel, there is no need to take a car. The town is built around its U-shaped harbor and it is easy to see the downtown area by walking or riding in a horse-drawn carriage. Jaunty little harbor ferries shuttle passengers around the harbor or on longer sightseeing tours. Double-decker buses for sightseeing and the trip to Butchart Gardens meet all arriving ships.

Getting to Victoria:

Crossing the Canadian/American border is usually not difficult: Some proof of American citizenship, such as a driver's license, voter's registration card, birth certificate, or passport, is required for adults, and proof of identity may be required for children.

Returning to the States, U.S. citizens are allowed $25 worth of articles per person for a stay of less than 48 hours, and $400 if the stay has been 48 hours or longer. For more information, pick up a **Customs** booklet at the Visitors Information office or call the U.S. Customs Office, 553-4676.

THE VICTORIA CLIPPER

Victoria Clipper's catamarans depart from Pier 69 in Seattle and take $1\frac{3}{4}$ to 3 hours to go to Victoria. These are passengers-only, no cars; reservations are required. A "cold meal basket," available for breakfast or dinner, costs $4.50-$6.50. There is a $5 surcharge each way for the fastest trip; prices for all trips are discounted in off-season.

Hours:	Departs Seattle: summer, 7:30am, 8am, 9am, 9:15am & 4pm; 2-3 trips daily spring & fall; winter 8am.
Cost:	Adults $55 one-way, $89 roundtrip. Seniors $49 one-way, $79 roundtrip. Children half price.
Phone:	448-5000, or 1-800-888-2535

THE ROYAL VICTORIAN

The only direct car ferry service between Seattle and Victoria is on Victoria Line's *Royal Victorian*. Based in Victoria, the *Royal Victorian* makes one roundtrip a day between the two cities, departing from Seattle at 1:00pm and from Victoria at 7:30am. The trip takes about $4\frac{1}{2}$ hours each way. The spacious ship has a gift shop and lounges, and serves a buffet meal in the dining room. Day rooms are available for an extra fee. Reservations required for vehicles.

Price:	Car & driver: $46.15 U.S. each way. Passengers: $21.80 each way. Children under 12: half-price. Under 5, free.

Phone: 1-604-480-5555 or
          1-800-683-7977.

Passengers may combine the trip and use the
Clipper one way and the *Royal Victorian* the
other; ask for the combination fare.

■ DRIVING/FERRY COMBINATIONS:

For a scenic trip, drive to Port Angeles on the
Olympic Peninsula (see the Olympic Peninsula
section, page 66). In Port Angeles, take a ferry to
Victoria — the **Black Ball ferry** *Coho* and, in the
summer, the *Victoria Express*. Allow about three
hours traveling time from downtown Seattle to
Port Angeles. Ferry schedules are available at
many places, including Visitor Information offices, hotels, and the Washington State Ferry
terminal at Pier 52.

The Seattle-Bainbridge Island ferry leaves
from Pier 52, takes 35 minutes to go to Winslow,
and has frequent departures. There are also the
Keystone-Port Townsend ferry and the **Ed-
monds-Kingston ferry**. See information on Cross-
Sound Ferries, pages 100-101 in the Ferry section,
or phone 464-6400 for information.

THE BLACK BALL FERRY

The Port Angeles-Victoria ferry trip on the
Black Ball Ferry takes 1 hour and 35 minutes and
makes four trips daily during the summer. Reservations are not accepted. If taking a car, arrive
early to be sure of getting on. There's cafeteria
service on all ferries. See page 67 for more information about Port Angeles.

Hours: Summer: 4 roundtrips daily.
          Fall: 2 trips daily.
          Winter: 1 trip daily.

Cost: Car & driver $27 U.S.
          Passengers or walk-ons
          one-way: adults $6.50,
          children 5-11, $3.25.

Phone: 622-2222, 360-457-4491

THE VICTORIA EXPRESS

Also leaving from **Port Angeles** is the Victoria Rapid Transit passenger ferry, the *Victoria Express*, which leaves from the Port Angeles Landing Mall and lands by Victoria's Regent Hotel. Trips take one hour; snacks and duty-free shopping are available on board. Reservations are accepted.

Hours:	Summer: 3 trips daily.
	Spring & fall: 2 trips daily.
Cost:	Adult $12.50 one-way,
	$20 roundtrip.
	Children 5-11, $7.50 one-way,
	$10 roundtrip.
	Seniors $11.50 one-way,
	$18 roundtrip.
	Under 5, free.
Phone:	1-800-633-1589 (in Washington) or 1-360-452-8088

There are three other water routes with scheduled service to Victoria, and others by charter. Regardless of the route, the scenery is spectacular.

ANACORTES-SIDNEY FERRY

A Washington State Ferry departs at 8am daily from Anacortes and stops at the San Juan Islands along the way to Sidney, B.C.; the trip takes three hours. During summer months an extra trip is added; reservations for cars are a must for these ferries. Note: This is the only Washington State ferry using reservations.

Driving to Anacortes from Seattle: Go north on I-5 to the Anacortes sign, exit #226 (Mt. Vernon), and head west to Anacortes. It's approximately 1¾ hours from Seattle to the ferry dock. Arrive early and be prepared to wait.

Cost:	Car and driver: one-way $29.70 ($35.65 summer).
	Passengers: Adults $6.90, children & seniors $3.45.
Phone:	464-6400

BC FERRIES

To the north, Canada's BC Ferries depart from **Tsawwassen**, southwest of Vancouver, and go through the Gulf Islands to Swartz Bay, just north of Sidney. The drive from Seattle to Tsawwassen takes approximately $2\frac{3}{4}$ hours with a normal border crossing. The ferry trip from Tsawwassen to Swartz Bay takes one hour 35 minutes, and the drive from Sidney south to Victoria takes approximately 45 minutes. Ferries leave hourly during the summer, less frequently other times; no reservations. Cafeteria service is available on all ferries.

Cost: Car and driver $33.50 Canadian (about $24 U.S.). Passenger $6.50 one-way. Children 5-11, $3.25 Canadian (about $2.25 U.S.). Both U.S. and Canadian currencies are accepted.

Phone: 1-604-656-0757

■ SEAPLANE

The fastest way to get to Victoria from downtown Seattle is by a seaplane from Lake Union. The planes land right in Victoria's Inner Harbour. Flight time is approximately 45 minutes.

KENMORE AIR

Kenmore Air has regularly scheduled flights from Lake Union daily in the summer and charter service available at all times. Reservations required.

Cost: Adults $83 one-way, $149 roundtrip

Phone: 486-1257 or 1-800-543-9595

Sound Flight, which flies out of the Renton Municipal Airport on the south end of Lake Washington, has chartered air service (phone 255-6500).

■ AIRPLANE

Horizon Airlines (phone 1-800-547-9308) and **Air BC** (1-800-776-3000) have scheduled daily service from Sea-Tac Airport to Victoria.

■ BUS

Bus service between Seattle and Victoria is available. Call **Gray Line**, phone 626-5208 or 1-800-426-7532; the **Anacortes Sea-Tac Airporter**, phone 1-800-448-8443; or Greyhound, (to Port Angeles or Vancouver) phone 1-800-231-2222.

For more information, call Discover BC, 1-800-663-6000; **Tourism Victoria**, 1-604-953-2033 (1-800-663-3883 for hotel reservations); or **Tourism Vancouver**, 1-604-683-2000.

WHIDBEY ISLAND

Whidbey Island's quiet charm makes it an ideal getaway spot for a short visit or a long vacation. The road along its rolling hills offers views of historic sites, the countryside and Puget Sound. A visit to the island's many bed and breakfast inns, located in the more rural southern part, is a good way to soak up Whidbey's bucolic scenery.

The free public transit system runs the length of the island. Buses go from the Clinton ferry landing in the south to Oak Harbor at the north end, making stops at the towns and Keystone ferry dock in between. To ride, wait at a bus stop and flag the bus down as it approaches. Buses come every hour weekdays, on a limited schedule Saturdays, and do not run on Sundays and holidays. Call Whidbey Island Transit, 1-360-678-7771, for information.

The short ferry ride from **Mukilteo** (exit #189 from I-5) disembarks at **Clinton** on the southeast end of Whidbey. The main road, Hwy 525, heads north from the ferry landing. Note: Highway signs are rare; check your maps before starting out and look for regular street signs to your destination.

About two miles from the ferry dock two roads lead to the picturesque town of **Langley**. Along Langley Road grape vines mark the small **Whidbey Island Winery**. The **Whidbey Island Brewing Company** is on the north end of downtown. Besides its views and waterfront park, Langley has attractive shops with merchandise reflecting the artistic talents of area residents,

To continue north, return to Hwy 525 by way of **Bayview**, pausing at **Freeland** where the bakery on the main street sells picnic lunches perfect for eating later at one of the many scenic spots on the island.

Approaching **Greenbank**, on the right just south of the Greenbank Store on Resort Road is a sign for the **Meerkert Rhododendron Gardens.** They are open year-round Wednesday-Sunday, 9am-4pm, and are especially beautiful in the spring when the rhododendrons are in bloom. The island's narrowest spot is Greenbank, known for its legendary loganberries. **Whidbey's Greenbank Farm** produces its liqueur from these berries, reputed to be the best, not only on the island, but in the world. The farm, owned by the same company that owns **Ste. Michelle Winery**, is open for free self-guided tours and wine (but not liqueur) tastings. It also has a gift shop and restrooms. The building and grounds are meticulously clean. A few miles north of Greenbank, the well-marked road to the **Keystone Ferry** landing and **Fort Casey State Park** branches off to the west. To go to the park, continue past the underwater preserve and around Crockett Lake to the park's entrance. Fort Casey's gun emplacements and **Admiralty Head Lighthouse** recall Whidbey Island's past at the turn of the century when it was part of the defense triangle on Puget Sound. Fort Casey has picnic and camping areas, steady breezes for kiteflying, and public restrooms (phone 360-678-4519).

Coupeville's historic Victorian homes, wharf and museum reflect the town's importance in the 19th century. The Na-

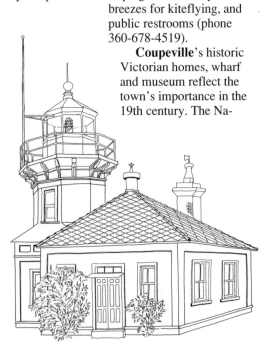

The Mukilteo lighthouse

tional Park Service exhibit at the foot of the wharf and the **Island County Historical Society Museum** (call for hours, 360-678-3310), just off Front Street, have information about the area's history. **Captain Whidbey's Inn**, one of the island's landmarks, is about three miles west of Coupeville, along Madrona Way.

Oak Harbor's proximity to the **U.S. Navy Air Station** has made it the island's largest city. A large windmill on the public beach is a reminder of its early Dutch settlers.

North of Oak Harbor, the road climbs into the forest and in a few minutes there are turn-offs for the parks, trails and campgrounds around **Deception Pass.** Pedestrians may cross the bridge to see dramatic views of the tidal currents far below.

For Visitor Information contact the **Whidbey Island Visitors Council**, P.O. Box 152, Coupeville, WA 98239; phone 360-678-5434, or in Langley, phone 360-221-6765. Also, visitor information is available through local chambers of commerce or privately operated concerns.

LA CONNER

La Conner, a small picturesque waterfront town with 19th-century ambiance, is a short detour on the way from Deception Pass heading east to I-5. Country shops and restaurants from casual to more elegant line the **Swinomish Slough**. For a look at the area's history, visit the restored Victorian **Gaches Mansion** on Second Street, usually open Friday-Sunday (phone 360-466-4288), and the **Historical Museum** on Fourth Street, open Wednesday-Sunday. The Museum of Northwest Art (phone 360-466-9133), showing contempory art, is on South First Street, next door to the La Conner Brewing Company (360-466-1415). Visitor information is available at the Chamber of Commerce office on First Street and Commercial in the Maple Center (phone 360-466-4778).

Bird lovers flock to the area year round. East of town, **Skagit Valley's** fertile fields are renowned for their tulips in the spring and berries and produce in the summer.

THE SAN JUAN ISLANDS

The San Juan Islands, known for their un-spoiled beauty, are one of Washington's most popular areas to visit in the summer. Many people explore the islands by boat, which enables them to search out secluded harbors and beaches. Others take a Washington State Ferry from Anacortes that stops at **Lopez, Shaw, Orcas**, and San Juan (at Friday Harbor) islands. The ferry trip is full of beautiful views of the smaller islands and sea life; whales may be seen swimming nearby.

During the summer, visitors overwhelm the ferry system and long waits are the norm, especially for passengers traveling with cars. Riders are advised to arrive at least an hour before the ferry's departure time, and even earlier on weekends. Driving time from Seattle to the Anacortes ferry dock is approximately $1\frac{3}{4}$ hours. The international ferry from Anacortes to Sydney, B.C., accepts reservations, but only in the summer; phone 1-800-542-7052 from Washington or 1-206-464-6400 from out of state. See the section on Ferries, pages 99-101, for more ferry information.

The first stop on most trips is **Lopez Island**, a favorite with bicyclists because of its gentle terrain. Near the ferry landing are a few shops and the Lopez Historical Museum; farther afield, the island has bed and breakfast inns and beautiful rural landscape to enjoy.

Shaw Island, the quietest of the San Juan islands with ferry service, has few public facilities. There is a store by the ferry dock — the dock is operated by nuns — and a public beach at Shaw Island County Park.

In contrast, public parks and tourist facilities abound on horseshoe-shaped **Orcas Island**. The road from the ferry landing goes in a half-circle to **Eastsound** in the middle and down the other side to **Olga**. Orcas has arts and crafts of all types in galleries and shops. The Artworks in Olga is a former strawberry processing plant turned into a cooperative of local artists.

The road continues through **Moran State
Park**, named after the industrialist who donated
the land for the park and built what is now the
Rosario resort. Inside the park, the road branches
to the left and goes six miles up **Mt. Constitu-
tion**, at 2,409 feet the highest spot in the islands —
a wonderful spot for views. The twisty road
makes for a scenic drive or a grueling bicycle ride.

   Friday Harbor, the islands' largest town, is
nestled around the San Juan Island ferry landing,
making it easy to visit without a car. Within walking distance of the ferry dock there are many
shops, restaurants and galleries on the main street

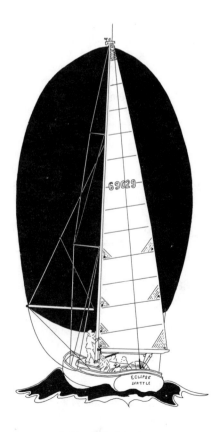

Sailing in the Islands

just beyond the dock and the **Whale Museum** is on First Street.

WHALE MUSEUM

Hours:	11am-4pm daily. Summer, 10am-5pm.
Cost:	Adults $4. Teens & seniors $3.50. Under 12, $1.00. Under 5, free.
Phone:	1-360-378-4710

The public **Whale Watching Park** is on the west side of the island, a 20-minute drive from Friday Harbor; several whale watching cruises are available; ask at Visitor Information.

Picturesque **Roche Harbor,** with its historic **Hotel de Haro** and gardens, is on the northwest coast of San Juan Island, approximately a half-hour drive from Friday Harbor. Nearby **English Camp**, a tranquil cove named for the troops quartered there in the mid-1800s, is now a national park, as is its counterpart at the south end of the island, **American Camp**, where the opposing American troops were bivouacked. The troops faced off only once, in a skirmish referred to as the **Pig War** in honor of its only casualty, as the countries debated the islands' ownership. In 1872 the lower islands became the American San Juans and the northern islands, Canada's **Gulf Islands**. The National Park Service presents programs at both English Camp and American Camp during the summer.

A word of warning: The San Juans' rural atmosphere belies their popularity. Plan ahead and make reservations if you plan to stay overnight on the islands in the summer. Prices below are for high season and are discounted in the off-season.

The two following tours, and travel to and from the San Juans may be broken up so that visitors may stay longer; be sure inquire when making reservations. In addition to the following tours, Friday Harbor's visitor information will have information about others.

ORCA WHALE SEARCH TOURS

Three-hour wildlife cruises with a professional naturalist look for Northwest ocean wild life: Daily at 11am, May - September.

Cost: Adults $20. Children $15.

Phone: 448-5000 or 1-800-888-2535

WATER TOUR

The Mosquito Fleet's San Juan Islands Sea-life Cruise, narrated by a marine biologist, departs from Everett and tours around the islands with a brief stop at Friday Harbor.

Cost: Adults $74.45. Seniors $63.66.
             17 & under, $42.08.

Phone: 206 252-6800

Getting to the San Juan Islands:

In addition to the Washington State Ferries, the *Victoria Clipper* has a daily trip from Pier 69 in Seattle to Friday Harbor and Rosario. Fares and schedules change, depending on the season. The **Island Shuttle Express**, also known as the **San Juan Foot Ferry**, has passenger-only service to the San Juans from Bellingham (phone 360-671-1137). It sails daily during the summer, stopping first on Orcas Island at Leiberhaven near Obstruction Pass and then at Friday Harbor on San Juan Island. See the Ferry section, pages 99-101, for more information.

Plane service to the islands is available. **Harbor Airlines** (phone 1-800-359-3220) has scheduled flights from Sea-Tac Airport to Friday Harbor. **Kenmore Air** provides regular seaplane service to the islands from Seattle and also charter air service to and beyond the islands (phone 486-8400).

Information about the San Juan Islands is available from the San Juan Islands Visitor Information Service, phone 360-468-3663.

LEAVENWORTH

When the coal mining and timber industries pe-
tered out in the 1960s Leavenworth turned itself
into a Bavarian village to capitalize on its marvelous physical setting. The Bavarian theme is perva-
sive, from the "Wilkommen in Leavenworth" sign
on the road, to the Bavarian style architecture, the
oom-pah music in the streets, and the merchandise
in the gift shops. There's even a small brewery,
Leavenworth Brewery (phone 509-548-4545),
on Front Street which serves pub food and has
daily tours. In addition, there are several popular
theme festivals during the year, such as **Oktober-
fest**, the **Autumn Leaf Festival**, the **Christmas
Lighting Festival** and **Maifest**.

Located in a narrow valley on the Cascade
Mountains' east side, the Leavenworth area is the
center for many outdoor activities, such as river
rafting, fishing, rock climbing and cross-country
skiing.

For more information, contact the Leavenworth Chamber of Commerce, P.O. Box 327,
703 Highway 2, Leavenworth, WA 98826
(phone 1-509-548-5807).

Getting to Leavenworth

From Seattle, head north on I-5 and take the
Bothell/Lake City exit, #171. The road becomes
Hwy 522; continue on 522 to Hwy 2 following
the signs to Stevens Pass. Leavenworth is 115
miles northeast of Seattle, approximately three
hours driving time.

PART II

AND MORE

The first chapters of *The Pocket Guide* cover Seattle by areas, since people often think in terms of a part of town, time frame, or distance when they sightsee.

This section has special interests — the pastimes, passions and necessities — that make up life in Seattle. It is organized alphabetically to make subjects easy to find.

As in the previous sections, boldfaced items are listed in the index.

AMUSEMENT PARKS

Seattle Center's Fun Forest is the only permanent amusement park in Seattle. The rides and booths open at noon and operate until midnight daily during the summer. Depending upon the weather they are open weekends during the spring and fall. Prices vary; entrance is free.

Hours: Noon-midnight (summer).

Phone: 684-7200

Enchanted Village, approximately half an hour south of Seattle on I-5, charges a park entry fee that includes rides. A combination ticket for Enchanted Village and the adjacent **Wild Waves Water Park** is available. Both are open only in the summer and have extended hours on weekends.

Hours: 10am-7pm (summer).

Phone: 1-206-661-8000

The **Seattle Funplex**, 1541 15th West, a little north of downtown Seattle on Elliott Avenue, is an indoor recreation and sports complex with an assortment of games for all ages. Open daily year-round.

Phone: 285-7842

ANNUAL EVENTS

Residents and visitors look forward to Seattle's many annual outdoor community events. In addition to listings below, many communities have celebrations, especially summer street fairs and markets. Check with local newspapers and visitors' information or the Washington State Department of Tourism. Admission is free unless noted.

OPENING DAY OF BOATING SEASON
First Saturday in May

A parade of boats — from decorated yachts to canoes — through the Montlake Cut, preceded by

University of Washington crew races. Sponsored by the Seattle Yacht Club (phone 325-1000).

FOLKLIFE FESTIVAL
Memorial Day weekend

A free four-day festival of arts and crafts, music, entertainers and food on the grounds of Seattle Center. Folklife publishes an annual ***Washington Festival Directory and Resource Guide***, available in stores or by mail (phone 684-7300).

PIONEER SQUARE FIRE FESTIVAL
First weekend in June

Old-time fire engines in Pioneer Square with appropriate noise to celebrate the 1889 fire that burned down pioneer Seattle and started its re-birth. Food, entertainers and Dalmations.

FOURTH OF JULY FIREWORKS
July 4

Seattle has two terrific fireworks shows:

AT&T sponsors the Family Fourth Fireworks show from Gasworks Park on Lake Union (phone 281-8111).

Ivar's sets off its fireworks from Myrtle Edwards Park at the north end of the Seattle waterfront (phone 587-6500).

BITE OF SEATTLE
Third weekend in July

A feeding frenzy with booths from 60-plus restaurants on the Seattle Center grounds. Prices per serving are in the $2-$5 range. Free entertainment; free admission (phone 232-2982).

PACIFIC NORTHWEST ARTS AND CRAFTS FAIR
Last weekend in July

The largest and best known of the many community arts and crafts fairs held throughout Seattle and the Northwest during the summer months. The official entries are in the west side of the Bellevue Square parking garage and the overflow surrounds Bellevue Square (phone 454-4900).

SEAFAIR
First weekend in August

Seafair is primarily known for its hydroplane boat races on the south end of Lake Washington and the **Torchlight Parade** held the preceding Friday, but it also includes many community events leading up to the races. Admission to the hydro races is $15; see page 118 (phone 728-0123).

BUMBERSHOOT
Labor Day weekend

Art displays and performances plus continuous, scheduled entertainment indoors and out throughout Seattle Center. Adults, $10; children under 12 and seniors, $1 (phone 281-7788).

WESTERN WASHINGTON STATE FAIR (THE PUYALLUP)
Middle three weeks in September

The largest of the state's many fairs with all the usual attractions, entertainers, and scones. Admission: $4-$6 (phone 206-845-1771).

CHRISTMAS SHIPS
Second week in December

Festive boats with carolers organized by three civic groups cruise Lake Union and Lake Washington before Christmas (phone 461-5840).

ART

Art abounds in Seattle! There's public art underfoot on the manhole covers, masquerading as chain link fences around the Safety Building's trees, and in grand statues like Henry Moore's *Three-Piece Vertebrae* at the 1001 Building on Fourth Avenue. The **City Centre** on Fifth and Pike has elegant glass pieces by Northwest artists in the upper lobby. Courtyards and corridors of the **Washington State Convention and Trade Center** at Eighth and Pike are filled with permanent and changing exhibits. **Seattle Center** has large outdoor pieces throughout its grounds — including its new musical fountain. Metro's tunnel stations are filled with art. Sea-Tac has art by local artists, and a balcony gallery with glass pieces.

Seattle's **"1% for Art"** program deserves thanks for most of our public art. In addition there are many shops, galleries and museums (see page 105) offering a wide variety of art.

Check local papers for current exhibits; a pamphlet listing shows in several galleries is available at Visitor Information booths. Many galleries open new exhibits and have an evening open house on the **First Thursday** of the month, when the Seattle Art Musuem is also free. The **Seattle Arts Commission** publishes a book available at bookstores and a free booklet with information about Seattle's public art.

Seattle manhole cover by Nathan Jackson

BREWERIES

Seattle has been in the forefront of the national trend for small craft breweries creating specialty brews. Several microbreweries catering to local beer connoisseurs have sprung up, not just in Seattle, but in outlying areas as well. A few, like Red Hook, have grown so much that they are no longer classified as microbreweries.

Most breweries offer tours and tastings and many taverns and restaurants have local micro-beers and ales on tap. There are three large beer festivals: The Cancer Lifeline Brewfest in April, the June Brewfest at the Herbfarm, and the Microbrew festival at Seattle Center in October, and also a **brew-pub tour**, call 763-BREW.

BIG TIME BREWERY & ALEHOUSE
4133 University Way

A busy brewpub in the University District, the Big Time serves three brews along with food. Open from 11:30am-12:30am, Sunday through Thursday, and 11:30am-1am on weekends.

Phone: 545-4509

HALE'S ALES, LTD.
4301 Leary Way NW

One of Washington's oldest breweris, Hale's recently moved from Kirkland to the Fremont area. The small brewing area has signs and de-scriptions of its brews for self-guided tours in the brewing area across from its pub. Open weekdays 11am-10pm, and 11am-midnight weekends.

Phone: 782-0737

HART BREWING
1201 1st Avenue So.

Hart brews both Pyramid Ales and Thomas Kemper Lagers at this new brewery just south of the Kingdome. Specialty brews are available on tap in the pub. Tours at 2 & 4pm. Open weekdays 11am-10pm, weekends 11am-11pm. Jammed be-fore and after Kingdome events.

Phone: 582-8322

KEMPER BREWING CO.
22381 Foss Road NE, Poulsbo

The original Kemper brewery is outside of Poulsbo on the Kitsap Peninsula. This small brew-ery and taproom is known for its hearty ales and authentic root beer. Open daily at 11am; tours at 2:30pm daily except Sunday.

Phone: 1-206-697-1446

MARITIME PACIFIC BREWING CO.
1514 NW Leary Way

A mini-brewery in Ballard, just off the Ballard Bridge. Open to the public for tastings Saturdays 11am-6pm and tours on the hour from 1-4pm.

Phone: 782-6181

McMENAMINS
200 Roy Street

Oregon's popular brewery has moved north and opened a couple of places in Seattle. This spot by Seattle Center is packed before and after Sonics games; the Six Arms on Capitol Hill is quieter. Both have small breweries, wine, and pub fare.

Phone: 285-4722

THE PACIFIC NORTHWEST BREWING COMPANY, LTD.
322 Occidental Avenue South

A spacious brewpub in Pioneer Square with pub fare and regular meal service. Its stunning antique brewing kettle is for decoration; the real brewing takes place in the back. Open evenings from 5pm; earlier Saturdays. Closed Sunday and Monday.

Phone: 621-7002

PIKE BREWING COMPANY
1415 First Avenue

Recently relocated to the South Arcade of the Market, this microbrewery shares its small space with Liberty Malt, a pub, and Seattle's Micro Brewery Museum. Open for sales and tastings 11am to 11pm Tuesday-Saturday, 11am to 5pm Sunday and Monday.

Phone: 622-1880

RAINIER BREWING COMPANY
3100 Airport Way South

Rainier Brewery, the area's largest brewery, is visible from I-5 just south of downtown Seattle. Open for guided tours and tastings Monday-Saturday, 1pm-6pm.

Phone: 622-2600

REDHOOK ALE BREWERY
3400 Phinney Avenue North

Redhook's brewery in the Fremont district was the first of the microbreweries and is the biggest. It has recently built another brewhouse on the Eastside, by the Columbia and Chateau Ste. Michelle wineries in Woodinville. Both breweries are open for tours (which cost $1) and tastings of its ales by reservation. The Trolleyman Pub next door in Fremont serves chili and pub fare, while the Woodinville pub serves box lunches for picnics on the grounds and has live music on weekends.

Phone: Fremont, 548-8000
           Woodinville, 483-3232

SEATTLE BREWERS
530 South Holden

Located in the industrial South Park area, this small brewery brews four distinctive ales. Open 3:30pm-7pm Monday-Friday for brewing, tasting.

Phone: 762-7421

WEST SEATTLE BREWERY
4720 California Avenue SW, West Seattle

The pub surrounds the brewing area of this small brewery, which brews its ales during the day. Pub open evenings.

Phone: 938-2476

BUSES AND VANS

Several companies provide scheduled service to destinations in the greater Seattle area and beyond; some stop only at the airport and not in downtown Seattle or vice versa.

Transportation from Seattle's **Sea-Tac International Airport** terminal to surrounding areas is available on Metro buses, taxis, shuttles or limousines. The shuttles leave from Sea-Tac's lower baggage level, usually stopping at the side parking lot at the airport's north end beyond United's baggage carousel #16, and five minutes later at the lot outside of baggage carousel #1. Reservations are required by some and generally recommended. Hotel vans pick up on the third floor of the parking garage.

For ground transportation information, call Sea-Tac's **Skyline**, 431-4444 or toll-free 1-800-544-1965, or **Ground Transportation**, 431-5906. Phone the carriers for specific schedule and fare information.

METRO

Metro buses serve the King County area, including the airport. To Sea-Tac, #194 is the express and #174 the local; both run about every half-hour and cost $1.10 or $1.60 depending on the time of day.

Phone: 553-3000

GRAY LINE

Gray Line's **Airporter** buses circle between Sea-Tac Airport and the major downtown hotels, leaving approximately every 15 minutes from 5am to midnight. They depart from the Gray Line booths in front of the terminal by baggage carousel #16 at the north end, and #3 at the south end.

Cost: $7.50 one-way.

Phone: 626-6088

GREYHOUND

The Seattle downtown terminal is on Stewart Street and Eighth Avenue for buses going throughout the country. At Sea-Tac Airport, Greyhound buses leave from the south end of the airport terminal, by baggage carousel #1.

Phone: 624-3456

QUICK SHUTTLE

Express bus service between Sea-Tac Airport or downtown Seattle (the Travelodge) and Vancouver, B.C. Six to eight trips daily.

Cost: $34 one-way from the airport;
          $28 from downtown.

Phone: 1-800-665-2122

SUPER SHUTTLE

Vans pick up at Sea-Tac Airport and serve King County and parts of Snohomish and Pierce Counties. Passengers must call for service with pick-up and drop-off information. Super Shuttle also has regularly scheduled runs to Mercer Island and the Eastside.

Cost: $18 and up, one-way,
          depending on distance.

Phone: 1-800-487-7433

COFFEE

Coffee connoisseurs love Seattle for the quantity of the purveyors and the quality of their brews. The aroma of freshly brewed coffee emanates from office buildings, stores and espresso carts on street corners in downtown Seattle. Every neighborhood has at least one place that makes espresso and lattes. Espresso bars and coffeehouses sell coffee from Northwest roasters by the cup or pound. Several are located in or near Pike Place Market and Pioneer Square, where tempting bakeries becken nearby.

Starbucks started the trend toward gourmet coffee in the 1980s; it is still the largest and has several coffee bars and shops throughout the Seattle area. Other roasters with shops in downtown are SBC, Torrefazione and Caffe D'arte; and there are other shops and carts throughout the area. Each has its devoted fans.

CURRENCY EXCHANGE

The main branches of downtown banks will exchange U.S. money for foreign currencies or vice versa; most banks are able to exchange Canadian-U.S. dollars. Some hotels will exchange currency, depending on their supply.

Thomas Cook (phone 623-6203) with locations in downtown Seattle, Bellevue, and the airport can exchange most currencies; call to be sure of availability. The downtown office is open weekdays only; Westlake Center is with the Information Desk, open and the Bellevue office is open weekdays and Saturdays. There are three booths at Sea-Tac Airport providing foreign exchange service; hours vary.

Check Mart, Inc. exchanges Canadian currency and will cash checks from a few foreign countries at their ten locations. Phone 622-2274.

American Express also has Canadian and other foreign funds available at the 600 Stewart Street office; open weekdays. Phone 441-8622.

THE EASTSIDE

Originally bedroom communities for Seattle, the Eastside is now one of Washington's fast-growing areas. Encompassing the cities east of Lake Washington, including Bellevue, Redmond, Woodinville, and Issaquah, the Eastside has been dubbed "Silicon Valley North." because of **Microsoft** and other high-tech companies located there. Still known for its suburban lifestyle, the area's commercial center is downtown Bellevue. Bellevue Square, an upscale mall, is downtown (see page 113), and there are other malls and shops throughout the area; also see Gilman Village, page 113. Several of the state's wineries are located on the Eastside (see pages 128-130), as well as Redhook Brewery, (page 93) and the tiny

Aviator Ale (phone 487-0717). A trip to **Sno-qualmie Falls** (pages 57-58) or the **Herbfarm** on the back roads is a great way to see the rural areas. The **Spirit of Washington** train travels the tracks from Renton to Woodinville (page 124) and the Lake Cruise explores Lake Washington.

For more information call the East King County Convention and Visitors Bureau, 455-1926.

ENTERTAINMENT/NIGHTLIFE

Seattle has a lively performing arts scene with resident symphony, ballet, and opera companies, as well as many theaters. For current information, check the daily newspapers and sources listed on pages 131-133.

Seattle boasts an abundance of theaters, performances and equity actors. There are major traveling shows, local theater seasons and small off-beat productions. The **University of Washington** has a large drama department and several performance stages; phone 543-4880 for information.

Ticketmaster sells tickets to area concerts and events (phone 628-0888 or 292-ARTS); they have ticket outlets in several Seattle stores and Westlake Center. The Westlake Center booth also sells discounted day-of-show tickets on a cash-only basis; call 233-1111. Some half-price day-of-show tickets are available through **TicketTicket**, located in the Broadway Market, 401 Broadway East, on Capitol Hill, and in the Pike Place Market Information booth (phone 324-2744).

For information about the **Seattle Symphony Orchestra** call 443-4747, for the **Seattle Opera** call 389-7676, and for **Pacific Northwest Ballet** call 292-2787.

For those looking for more casual entertainment, many places in Pioneer Square have bands or performers. Other areas to try are the restaurants around the south end of Lake Union and out by Shilshole. Local rock bands playing the "Seattle Sound" play at clubs and halls. Comedy clubs have sprung up all over the city. And most of the major hotels have lounges with music and dancing.

FACTS AND TRIVIA

Like other parts of the country, our corner has its own personality and quirks. For instance:

Seattle has only 55 clear days a year. The rest range from partly cloudy to steady rain, although we have only about 36 inches of rain a year.

People buy more pairs of sunglasses per capita in Seattle than any other city — probably because it's so long between sunny days that people forget where they've put their glasses. We also buy more cars with sunroofs — so we can see the sun when it comes out.

Seattleites are readers — we use the public library more and buy more books than people in other cities. It follows that we also have more bookstores selling both new and used books. Could be because there's a high percentage of college graduates here — or because the gray days are perfect for curling up with a good book.

And we love our theaters! We have more equity theaters and performances in Seattle than any city except New York and Chicago.

We're concerned about the environment — 90% of Seattle residents dutifully separate their trash for curbside recycling, one of the best records in the country.

Those bikeracks you see on the front of Metro's buses are there for a reason— Seattle has the highest percentage of people biking to work in the country.

Seattle's monorail was the first full-scale monorail in the world when it was built for the 1962 World's Fair. It carries more than two million people a year between Seattle Center and downtown.

Local lore has it that Seattle was built on seven hills, but there are several versions of what those seven are, and one of them, Denny, was sluiced into Elliott Bay and is now a flatland. The granite slabs in Westlake Park are symbollic of our hills

Seattle's revered pioneers are buried on a knoll in Lake View Cemetary on Capitol Hill. Nearby, and much more frequently visited, is the grave of martial arts star **Bruce Le**e.

If you're confused about downtown street names, remember: **J**esus **C**hrist **M**ade **S**eattle **U**nder **P**rotest. That mnemonic helps with street names starting in Pioneer Square and heading north. The streets are: Jefferson, James, Cherry, Columbia, Marion, Madison, Spring, Seneca, University, Union, Pike and Pine.

Thanks to a ruling by the U.S. Supreme Court that declared New York's Long Island wasn't technically an island, Whidbey Island is the longest island in the country.

FERRIES

The **Washington State Ferry** fleet is the largest in the nation — its 24 ships carry more than 22 million passengers a year across Puget Sound. Riding a ferry is part of the daily commute for many Washingtonians; it is also an excellent way for visitors to get out on the water and see some of the state's beautiful scenery.

To ride a ferry as a walk-on passenger, be at the ferry terminal 10-15 minutes before departure, buy a ticket and walk on when the ferry is ready. Passengers pay only on the Seattle (east) side.

To go with a vehicle, allow more time, especially on weekends and during commuter hours. Vehicles are loaded in order of arrival; once your car is in line you might explore the Waterfront. There are no reservations on Washington State Ferries except on the **Anacortes-Sydney** ferry during the summer (see the Victoria section, page 69). Some private ferries accept reservations.

Two car ferries leave from **Pier 52** on the Seattle waterfront. The trip to **Winslow** on **Bainbridge Island** is aboard one of the jumbo ferries, the newest and largest in the fleet. Ferries between Seattle and Winslow leave approximately every hour. The crossing takes 35 minutes, a roundtrip takes about $1\frac{1}{2}$ hours. Ferries between Seattle and **Bremerton** are slightly less frequent; the crossing takes one hour, a roundtrip takes about $2\frac{1}{2}$ hours. The ferries are large and comfortable and offer cafeteria service and great coffee.

The terminal on Pier 52 has a small restaurant, bar, T-shirt shop, and very small restrooms; a McDonald's is on the street level. The grand old clock from the original **Colman Dock** is on display. The information desk in the terminal is open from 7:30am to 6:30pm. Ferry schedules are available at the terminal and Visitor Information Centers throughout the Seattle area.

■ CROSS-SOUND FERRIES

Cost: Passengers, one-way *or* round-trip: Adults $3.50.
Children 5-11 & seniors $1.75.
Auto & driver $5.90 *each* way.
Car fares are $7.10 each way in the summer.

Phone: 464-6400 or 1-800-84-FERRY.

Next door on Pier 50, the state's two passenger-only ferries leave for **Bremerton** and **Vashon Island**. Tickets may be purchased at the pier.

Washington State Ferry routes for other ferries are shown on most Washington State maps. All

The Washington State ferry Vashon

the ferry trips are scenic with views of Puget Sound and its islands, but the most popular is the trip through the **San Juan Islands.** Ferries depart from **Anacortes,** approximately 1¾ hours drive northwest of Seattle, and sail to four of the islands. Extra sailings are added for the peak season. Allow plenty of time; the ferries are jammed in the summer, especially on weekends.

Cost: Varies depending upon destination.

Phone: 464-6400 or 1-800-84-FERRY

■ PRIVATE FERRY LINES

In addition to the state ferry system, several private lines serve other communities:

SEATTLE - VICTORIA

For information on ferry service to **Victoria, B.C.** — the *Victoria Clipper* and the *Royal Victorian* from Seattle, and the *Victoria Express* and **Black Ball** from Port Angeles — see the section on Victoria, pages 69-73.

BREMERTON - PORT ORCHARD

Washington's shortest ferry trip is the 10-minute journey between Bremerton and Port Orchard. Known locally as the foot ferry, the boat departs at quarter-to and quarter-past the hour from its dock across the parking lot from the Seattle-Bremerton ferry dock. Passengers and bicycles only.

Cost: $1.00 each way.

Phone: 1-360-876-2300

BELLINGHAM - SAN JUAN ISLANDS

The **Island Shuttle Express,** known as **The San Juan Foot Ferry,** sails daily during the summer from Bellingham to Friday Harbor on San Juan Island and Leiberhaven on Orcas Island. Passengers and bicycles only.

Cost: $20 one-way; $33 roundtrip.

Phone: 360-671-1137

BELLINGHAM - ALASKA

The Alaska ferry sails from Bellingham, departing from the **Alaska Marine Highway Terminal, Pier 48**. Reservations required; call 1-360-676-8445 or 1-800-642-0066. For Bellingham Visitor Information call 1-360-671-3990.

FISH

For those who want to buy some of Washington's celebrated seafood, there are several fish markets in Pike Place Market, the Wild Salmon at Fisherman's Terminal, and many throughout the greater Seattle area listed in the Yellow Pages under "Fish." Most will pack fresh seafood to travel. Note: It's a good idea to carry perishable items with you on planes rather than checking them with the luggage.

FISHING

A **license** is required for persons 16-69 to fish for most species in Washington. The Department of Wildlife issues licenses for inland waters and the Department of Fisheries issues licenses for saltwater species. Both licenses may be purchased at area drug, hardware, and sporting goods stores. Prices vary depending on residency, time period, and species. For information call the Washington State Department of Fish and Wildlife, 1-360-902-2200; in King County call 206-775-1311.

FREE — OR ALMOST

Some of the best things to do in Seattle are free or charge a minimal fee. Most places offer discounts for groups; it's best to call ahead. See the following Garden Section and the View Section, page 124, for other ideas.

The **Waterfront Streetcar** — It's not free, but it charges Metro's rates, $.85 regular fare, or $1.10 at peak hours, and the tickets allow passengers to get off and on for an hour. The colorful trolleys go from the north end of the Waterfront to the International District. See page 6.

The **Metro Ride Free Bus Zone** downtown. See page 5.

The **Metro Tunnel** — Not only is it free and a terrific way to go from one end of downtown to the other, but it's beautiful as well. See page 5.

The **Monorail** — Ninety cents a person, $.60 for kids, each way from Westlake Center to Seattle Center. See pages 7 and 31

Some bus routes are perfect for sightseeing: #43 covers the University District and the Arboretum; #46 goes through Ballard, by the Locks and out to Shilshole; #37 wends its way from downtown over to West Seattle and Alki Beach.

The **Washington State Ferries** — A roundtrip ride costs about $3.50 for a walk-on passenger, depending on the route. See page 98.

The **Klondike Gold Rush National Park** or **Museum** in Pioneer Square. See page 25.

The **Smith Tower** — The ride to the 35th floor in the elegant brass elevator costs $2 and then the ornate **Chinese Throne Room** and the spectacular view of city are free. See page 25.

Summer **Out to Lunch** concerts and performances in downtown parks and courtyards.

The Tour Section, page 120, lists several free tours, also see area **wineries,** page 128, and **breweries**, page 90.

The **Hiram A. Chittenden Locks**, see page 39.

Most museums have a free or discounted day; call to inquire. See page 105.

GARDENS

With Seattle's mild, moist climate, plants and flowers flourish. Here are some favorite public gardens.

Woodland Park Rose Garden adjacent to the Woodland Park Zoo, page 45.

The **University of Washington** campus; the roses by the **Drumheller Fountain**, page 46.

The **Washington Park Arboretum**, page 48.

The **Carl S. English, Jr. Gardens** at the Locks, page 39.

The **Japanese Garden** in the Arboretum, page 49.

The grounds of **Seattle Center**, pages 31-36.

Volunteer Park; the **Conservatory** in the park; and the **dahlia** (Seattle's official flower) display southeast of the Conservatory.

Bellevue's Botanical Garden, 12001 Main Street, a new public garden with Northwest plants and a separate Japanese Garden. Phone 462-2749.

The **Community Arboretum** on the South Seattle Community College campus overlooking Puget Sound. Phone 764-5336.

The **Herbfarm** in Fall City. See page 58.

The **Bloedel Reserve** on **Bainbridge Island.** Open Wednesday through Sunday. Phone 1-206-842-7631 for reservations and directions.

The **Kubota Garden** in the Rainier Beach area is a blend of traditional Japanese garden concepts with native Northwest plant material.

The **Rhododendron** and **Bonzai Gardens** at **Weyerhaeuser** headquarters in Federal Way. Call 1-206-838-4646 for prices and hours.

INTERPRETERS/TRANSLATORS

A.C.E. (American Cultural Exchange) offers professional interpretation and translation services for individuals and businesses; phone 281-8200.

ATS, Accurate Translation Services, offers document translation; phone 778-4626.

The **American Red Cross** provides volunteer interpreters who are able to translate 70 languages and dialects for people needing assistance. Volunteers are available 24 hours a day through the **Red Cross Language Bank**; phone 323-2345.

MEDICAL CARE

For emergencies, call 911.

Medical care is available through area hospitals and organizations.

Hospital emergency rooms throughout the greater Seattle area are open 24 hours a day. Several are located just outside the downtown area; check the Yellow Pages listings under "Hospitals."

For less traumatic illnesses, there are clinics and medical centers. Hours and prices vary; it's a good idea to call beforehand to be sure they can meet your needs.

The **Downtown Clinic**, Medical Dental Building at Fifth and Olive, Suite 1664, in downtown Seattle. Hours: Monday-Friday, 8am-5pm; Saturday, 9am-1pm. Phone 682-3808.

Virginia Mason Fourth Avenue Clinic, 1221 Fourth Avenue, offers general health services and a walk-in clinic. Phone 223-6490.

CHEC Medical Centers have several locations throughout the greater Seattle area. In downtown Seattle there is a clinic at Denny and Fairview Avenue. Phone 682-7418.

MUSEUMS

Pursue a special interest or explore a niche in history through a trip to one of the area's many museums. Most are closed one day a week (Monday usually) and offer free admission on certain days. Call to check on directions, hours, prices and exhibits. Unless noted, the museums are in Seattle.

In addition to the museums listed below, there are galleries featuring works of art in all media, many clustered in the Pioneer Square area — see the Art section, page 89.

BELLEVUE ART MUSEUM
Third Floor, Bellevue Square, Bellevue

A spacious museum exhibiting special shows, often featuring Northwest artists. Gift shop.

Phone: 454-6021

BREMERTON NAVAL MUSEUM
130 Washington Street, Bremerton

Ship models, weapons and artifacts from the U.S. Navy, overlooking the Navy shipyards.

Phone: 1-206-479-SHIP

BURKE MUSEUM
Northwest corner, University of Washington

Northwest Native American and natural history exhibits. Gift store and coffee shop. See page 46.

Phone: 543-5590

THE CENTER FOR WOODEN BOATS
1010 Valley Street

Part museum, part boat rentals, this is a favorite stop for sailors and rowers who take classic crafts out on the water.

Phone: 382-2628

CHILDREN'S MUSEUM
Lower floor, Center House, Seattle Center

Hands-on neighborhoods for young explorers, plus changing shows. Gift shop. See page 33.

Phone: 298-2521

COAST GUARD MUSEUM
Pier 36, 1519 Alaskan Way South

Collection of Pacific Northwest Coast Guard memorabilia, including uniforms and guns. Free.

Phone: 217-6993

FRYE ART MUSEUM

707 Terry Avenue

The grande dame of private Seattle art museums has been recently remodelled and enlarged. Permanent and changing fine art exhibits.

Phone: 622-9250

HENRY ART GALLERY

15th Avenue, University of Washington

Closed until 1997 for remodelling.

Phone: 543-2280

HYDROPLANE AND RACEBOAT MUSEUM

1605 So. 93rd Street

Historic boats and memorabilia from years of Seattle's hydro races in a working shop where they are restored. Open Thursdays and Saturdays. Free.

Phone: 764-9453

KINGDOME SPORTS MUSEUM

201 So. King Street at the Kingdome

Open during Kingdome events or tours. See page 28.

Phone: 296-3128

KLONDIKE GOLD RUSH MUSEUM

117 South Main Street, Pioneer Square

Exhibits of the Klondike Gold Rush and the role Seattle played in it. Free. See page 25.

Phone: 553-7220

MARYMOOR MUSEUM

Marymoor Park, Redmond

The history, crafts, and businesses, including the recently arrived high tech companies, of the communities on the east side of Lake Washington.

Phone: 885-3684

MUSEUM OF FLIGHT
9404 East Marginal Way South

Elegant building filled with planes and other flying contraptions and their history. Museum store. See page 51.

> Phone: 764-5720

MUSEUM OF HISTORY AND INDUSTRY
2700 24th Avenue East

Puget Sound history, with exhibits of a pioneer street, the Great Seattle Fire, and changing exhibits showing Seattle's devolment. Lots of memorabilia from past events. Gift shop.

> Phone: 324-1125

NORDIC HERITAGE MUSEUM
3014 NW 67th Street, Ballard

Exhibits depicting the Scandinavian heritage in Puget Sound, including a recreated early village and fishing lore. Gift shop.

> Phone: 789-5707

PACIFIC SCIENCE CENTER
200 Second Avenue, Seattle Center

Hands-on exhibits, displays, movies and changing shows. Restaurant and gift shop. See page 34.

> Phone: 443-2001

ROSALIE WHYEL MUSEUM OF DOLL ART
1116 108th Avenue NE, Bellevue

Historic dolls, teddy bears and toys displayed in vignettes in an elegant Victorian setting. Changing exhibits and store.

> Phone: 455-1116

SEATTLE ART MUSEUM
First & University, downtown

Known locally as **SAM**, Seattle's largest fine arts museum is in its stunning new building downtown. Permanent exhibits of Asian, African and Northwest art, plus changing shows. Gift shop. The **Seattle Asian Art Museum (SAAM)** is in the original Volunteer Park building.

Phone: 625-8900

SNOQUALMIE VALLEY HISTORICAL MUSEUM

320 So. North Bend Boulevard, North Bend

Displays of Snoqualmie Valley and Snoqualmie Pass history. Closed in winter. See page 58.

Phone: 1-206-888-3200

SUQUAMISH MUSEUM

Highway 305 on the Olympic Peninsula, just west of the Agate Pass Bridge

Exhibits and pictures tell the history of Puget Sound's Native Americans. See page 65.

Phone: 1-206-598-3311

WING LUKE ASIAN MUSEUM

407 Seventh Avenue South

Exhibits, crafts and photographs of Seattle's Asian heritage. Gift shop. See page 30.

Phone: 623-5124

The Seattle Art Museum

PARKS

The **Olmsted Brothers** firm of Massachusetts designed a grand plan for Seattle's parks at the turn of the century and, although not all of it was built, most of Seattle's extensive park system is part of the "Olmstead Legacy." **Volunteer Park** the **University of Washington** campus, and the **Arboretum** are Olmstead parks, as is the parkway along the shore of Lake Washington. There are large city parks, such as **Seattle Center**, view parks along the waterfronts and on hillsides, and many small pocket parks. There are one-of-a-kind parks, like **Gasworks**, a unique park created from an industrial eyesore; **Discovery Park**, a wilderness park; and the **Japanese Garden**, to name a few. Many have jogging trails — like **Green Lake**, the city's most heavily used park, which makes it the best for people-watching.

The Parks Department supports a broad range of activities at various parks — from pleasant walks and views to playing golf, renting boats, and classes.

For information, call the **Seattle Parks and Recreation Department.**

Phone: 684-4075

PHONES

All Western Washington used to have area code 206, but now it's split, with the Greater Seattle area retaining 206 and outlying areas now using 360. Because of heavy demand, there may be another one added soon.

Phone cards are available at many downtown locations, including the Washington State Convention and Trade Center by Visitor Information.

RESTAURANTS

With an abundance of good restaurants in Seattle, selecting one is not easy. Restaurants are known for their Northwest fare, which emphasizes local seafood and fresh ingredients. In addition, there is a vast selection of ethnic restaurants ranging from Mexican and Italian to Santa Fe style and Czechoslovakian. Here are some resources for finding a place to eat.

The newspapers, including the free papers, have weekly restaurant reviews, and Friday's and Saturday's papers feature synopses of past reviews. Publications available at hotels (see page 131) such as *Where, Guest Informant,*and *Quick Guide* have lists of restaurants in various categories such as price or cuisine.

Some areas have a concentration of restaurants: Many small ethnic places are clustered in and around the **Pike Place Market** on Western and First Avenues. The **Pioneer Square** area has all kinds of restaurants and taverns and the **International District** has a wide variety of Asian restaurants — Japanese, Chinese, Thai, etc. Seafood places on the piers along the Waterfront range from casual fish and chips to the more elegant, and are jammed in the summer. Excellent restaurants are located in hotels and office buildings. For water views, try the restaurants around Lake Union; Shilshole Bay also has several places with stunning sunset views.

SHOPPING

Stores and boutiques abound in downtown Seattle offering everything from designer clothing to surplus materials. The major stores, **Nordstrom** and **The Bon Marché**, surround the landscaped brick plaza at **Westlake Park.** Below ground, the Metro Tunnel connects the stores with **Westlake Center**, a four-floor mall of shops and restaurants; open 9:30am to 8pm (phone 467-1600). Visitor information and a **Thomas Cook** currency exchange are on the main floor. The top floor has the southern **Monorail** terminal, a balcony overlooking the park, eating areas and restrooms.

Specialty shops line Fifth and Sixth Avenues and the side streets: City Centre on Union has Barney's and F.A.O. Schwarz; the glitzy new

Nike Town, Levi Strauss and Planet Hollywood
are across the street. Eddie Bauer and **Rainier
Square** are farther south on Fifth Avenue at
University Street. (Note: The walls of the Underground Concourse from One Union Square to
Rainier Square are covered with historical photographs of Seattle.)

There are many boutique-type shops in **Pioneer Square** and near the **Pike Place Market** on
First Avenue. The piers on the **Waterfront** are
chockablock with souvenir shops. In addition,
there are many shops in the major office towers
and tucked in among the buildings.

For shopping beyond downtown, near the
University of Washington campus there are
shops and restaurants all along University Avenue, known locally as **"The Ave."** The **University
Book Store,** one of the country's largest, is located between 44th and 45th Streets on University
Avenue. **University Village** is a shopping complex east of the university. The diverse population
of **Capitol Hill** is reflected in the eclectic boutiques and restaurants that line Broadway and fill
the **Broadway Market**. The **Fremont District**
across the Fremont Bridge is known for its funky
shops, restaurants and bars (see page 41).

There are three major **shopping malls,** each
about a half-hour drive from downtown Seattle.
Each of the malls has major department stores,
many smaller stores, and several restaurants. The
hours listed below are normal operating hours but
may change; it's a good idea to check.

NORTHGATE

Northgate was one of the country's first shopping centers and continues to thrive. Head north
on I-5 to the Northgate Way exit at 103rd Street,
exit #173; the mall is straight ahead on the east
side of the freeway.

Hours:	10am-9:30pm Mon-Sat; 11am-6pm Sun.
Phone:	362-4777

SOUTHCENTER

Southcenter, not far from Sea-Tac Airport, is one of the country's largest shopping centers. Head south on I-5 and exit at the Southcenter exit, #154. The shopping center is on the east side of the freeway. The retail area extends far beyond the shopping center complex.

Hours:	10am-9:30pm Mon-Sat; 11am-6pm Sun.
Phone:	246-7400

BELLEVUE SQUARE

Bellevue Square stores cater to the affluent Eastside. Drive east on either SR 520 or I-90 and get off at the Bellevue Way exit; follow Bellevue Way to downtown Bellevue. Bellevue Square covers the blocks between Bellevue Way and 100th Avenue, and between Eighth and Fourth Streets.

Hours:	9:30am-9:30pm Mon-Sat; 11am-6pm Sun.
Phone:	454-2431

GILMAN VILLAGE

Issaquah's Gilman Village's shops are housed in a cluster of turn-of-the-century buildings linked by a boardwalk. The small shops feature hand-crafted items, antiques and clothes; the restaurants feature homemade breads and soups. Beyond Gilman Village is a vast suburban sprawl of stores.

Take I-90 heading east to the Front Street exit, #17, in Issaquah; bear right onto Front Street, then turn right at the next intersection onto Gilman Boulevard, and continue about $\frac{1}{4}$ mile to Gilman Village on the left.

Hours:	10am-6pm Mon-Sat; 11am-5pm, Sun.
Phone:	462-0594

In the past few years several discount shopping malls have sprung up in outlying areas. The closest are the Factory Outlet Stores in Northbend and the **SuperMall** in Kent.

SPORTS

Sports are part of the Northwest life. On good days, bicyclers and joggers fill the trails, while boaters take to the waters. Even when the weather isn't inviting, people put on their waterproof clothes and enjoy outdoor activities.

■ BICYCLING

Seattle, Mercer Island, Bellevue, the Kitsap Peninsula, Whidbey Island, and the San Juan Islands all have trail maps for bicycling. Call their Visitor Information with questions. Bikes may be rented on the Waterfront at Pier 54. **Terrene Tours** has bicycle tours, with or without guides, and rents bikes; phone 325-5569.

■ CLIMBING

The Northwest's rugged geography has enticed rock climbers for years. More recently, man-made rocks have been built, the first at Camp Long in West Seattle in 1937; more recently one on the University of Washington campus and, the tallest, in Marymore Park in Redmond. An off-shoot has developed with several indoor climbing walls and clubs open; commuters may watch climbers at R.E.I.'s new store on Stewart Street.

■ SKIING

Seattle's gentle rains become snow at the higher elevations of the nearby mountain passes, enticing skiers to the Cascades from Thanksgiving to April for the accessible, often excellent, skiing.

There are four ski areas less than an hour's drive on I-90 from downtown Seattle; all have night skiing, equipment rentals, lodge and restaurant facilities. There are some overnight accommodations. The areas on the east side of the Cascades boast about their dry snow. In addition, there are several areas for cross-country skiing and some have facilities for downhill, cross-country and snowboarding. Equipment rentals and lessons are available at most areas; call for information.

It's hard to tell what the weather is in the mountains, so it's a good idea to call to confirm hours of operation and conditions.

The **Cascade Snowline** has recorded information for all the ski areas in the Cascades; phone 634-0200. For current **highway conditions** in the Cascades from November through March phone 455-7900. Note: Reports often state that approved traction devices are required; these include all-weather tires, snow tires and studded tires. Occasionally, chains are required.

For information about other ski areas in Washington, phone 1-206-586-2088.

Listed ticket prices are for the 1996 season, adult all-day tickets only. All areas offer different tickets for children, half-days, and nights.

SNOQUALMIE PASS

The Snoqualmie Pass areas are the closest to Seattle, approximately a one-hour drive east on I-90 from downtown Seattle. Snoqualmie Summit, Ski Acres, Hyak and Alpental are owned by one parent company known as **The Pass** and one lift ticket is good at all four areas. Night skiing is available every night, but nights vary with areas. On weekends a free bus shuttles skiers from one area to another. Each has its own restaurants, rental services, ski schools and other amenities. Snowboarding is allowed at all four areas and there are special snowboard parks at Snoqualmie Summit and Hyak. A tubing area is by Hyak.

Alpental, with 2,200 feet of vertical drop, has long, steep runs and spectacular scenery.

Snoqualmie Summit has gentle terrain and caters to beginning skiers.

Ski Acres has 1,020 feet of vertical drop and offers a broad range of skiing.

Hyak, the farthest east of the areas, has mostly intermediate terrain. It is open only on weekends.

Cost:	$28 weekends; $14 Mon & Tues; $16 Wed-Thurs; $18 Fri.
Phone:	232-8182; ski report, 236-1600

Cross Country Skiing: Ski Acres' Cross-Country Center includes two tracks with areas lighted for night skiing and full facilities.

Cost: $5; or $9 with two roundtrip chairlift rides.

Getting to Snoqualmie Pass:

Limited bus service from downtown Seattle and surrounding areas is available. Call for information, 232-8210.

Driving directions: Head east on I-90 to exit #52 (West Summit) for Alpental and Snoqualmie or exit #53 (East Summit) for Ski Acres and exit #54 for Hyak.

CRYSTAL MOUNTAIN

Crystal Mountain, Washington's largest ski area, has a 3,100-foot vertical drop, two new quad chairlifts, and extensive, varied terrain. On a clear day the view of nearby Mt. Rainier is breathtaking. Crystal has full facilities and some overnight accommodations. Limited night skiing. Cross-Country Skiing: Crystal Mountain has some terrain suitable for cross-country skiing.

Cost: $33 weekends; $20 Mon & Tues; $24 Wed-Fri.

Phone: 1-360-663-2265; ski report, 634-3771

Getting to Crystal Mountain:

The drive from Seattle takes $1\frac{3}{4}$ hours. Bus transportation is available from outlying areas to Crystal; phone 626-5208.

Driving directions: Head southeast to Enumclaw (there are several roads) and continue east on Rte 410.

STEVENS PASS

Stevens Pass, on the road to Leavenworth, has an 1,800-foot vertical drop, extensive terrain, night skiing and full facilities.

Cost: $32 weekends; $16 Mon & Tues; $24 Wed-Fri.

Phone: 1-360-973-2441;

ski report, 634-1645

Cross Country Skiing: The Stevens Pass Nordic Center is five miles beyond Stevens on Mill Valley; open Friday-Sunday.

Cost $7.50

Getting to Stevens Pass:

From downtown Seattle, go across Lake Washington and head north on I-405 to the Monroe/ Wenatchee exit, #23, and continue east on SR 2. Driving time from Seattle is approximately 1¾ hours.

Other areas with facilities for **cross-country** skiing include:

MOUNT RAINIER

There are three marked trails from **Paradise**, and the **Ski Touring Center at Longmire** offers rentals, lessons and advice for areas around Mount Rainier.

Cost: $5 park entrance fee.

Phone: 1-206-569-2283

■ OTHER SPORTS

For information about fishing, see page 102. For water activities, see pages 127.

SPECTATOR SPORTS

Seattle has teams for all seasons, indoors and out. For ticket information and game schedules, call the numbers listed or the resources in the back of the guide. Tickets for most events are also available through **Ticketmaster** (phone 628-0888). Metro schedules extra buses for some events; for information call 553-3000.

■ EMERALD DOWNS

Thoroughbred horse racing, June to November, has returned to the Seattle area in Auburn; phone 1-888-931-8400.

■ EVERETT AQUASOCS

A farm team for the Mariners, this Class A team plays outdoor games at the Everett Memorial Stadium from June to September; call 206-258-3673.

■ MARINERS

The Mariners, Seattle's American League baseball team, play their home games in the Kingdome from April to October.

Phone: 628-3555 or 622-HITS

■ SEADOGS

Seattle's indoor soccer team, the SeaDogs play their CISL games at the KeyArena from June to September; call 281-5800.

■ SEAFAIR

Seattle's annual Seafair festival culminates in the **Unlimited Hydroplane Races** the first Sunday in August on Lake Washington south of the Mercer Island Floating Bridge (I-90). Thousands of people watch from boats on the water. **Seward Park** at the south end of Lake Washington is where the landlubbers go.

Cost: $15.
Phone: 728-0123

■ SEAHAWKS

The Seahawks, Seattle's NFL football team, play their home games at the Kingdome.

Phone: 827-9766

■ SOUNDERS

Major league soccer has returned to Seattle with the APSL Sounders. Games are played in the summer in Memorial Stadium.

Phone: 622-3415 or
           1-800-796-KICK

■ SUPERSONICS

Home games of the SuperSonics, Seattle's NBA basketball team, are played in the KeyArea (formerly the Coliseum) at Seattle Center. The regular season runs November through April.

    Phone: 281-5850

■ TACOMA RAINIERS

The Mariners AAA farm team, the Rainiers play their games outdoors at the Cheney Stadium from April to September; call 1-800-281-3834.

■ THUNDERBIRDS

The Thunderbirds compete against other young teams in the Western Hockey League from October to March. Games are played at Seattle Center, usually in the Arena; some are in the KeyArena.

    Phone: 728-9121

■ UNIVERSITY OF WASHINGTON

UW football games in Husky Stadium are usually sold out, but tickets are generally available for basketball and other sports in the Hec Edmundson Pavilion. Spectators flock to the Montlake Cut to watch the annual Opening Day crew races preceding the **Opening Day Boat Parade** (see page 87).

    For University of Washington sports information phone 543-2200.

TOTEM POLES

    Although local Puget Sound Indians did not carve totem poles, the spectacular monuments created by tribes farther north have become a symbol of the Northwest's Indian heritage. Many may be found in and around Seattle:

Pioneer Square Park, the triangular park at First Avenue and Yesler Way by the pergala.

Occidental Park, on Occidental Avenue between Washington and Main Streets.

Alaska Square, the small park on the Waterfront at the foot of Washington Street. See page 16.

The Seattle Art Museum, Northwest Coast Native American Collection. See page 108.

Seattle Center, near the Mural Amphitheatre.

The Burke Museum, 17th Avenue NE and NE
45th Street, on the University of Washington
campus, both inside and out. See page 46.

Victor Steinbrueck Park, on the water side of
the Pike Place Market overlooking Elliott Bay, at
Virginia Street and Western Avenue.

At the east entrance of the **Montlake Cut** on the
south bank; just north of the **Museum of History
and Industry**'s upper parking lot.

Ivar's Salmon House on Lake Union.

Daybreak Star Cultural Center in Discovery
Park. See page 42.

Tillicum Village on Blake Island. See page 21.

The **Suquamish Museum** on Rte 305 west of
Winslow. See page 65.

Belvedere Viewpoint, Admiral Way at SW Olga
Street in West Seattle.

By the entrance to **Northgate Shopping Center**.
See page 112.

TOURS AND SIGHTSEEING

Many area attractions offer tours of their facilities; some are free, while others have an admission charge. Most offer discounts or will arrange
special tours for groups. Availability may change,
so call to verify before setting out.

In addition to the tours listed below, check the
Breweries and Wineries sections; many have regular tours or will do tours upon request.

THE ARBORETUM
See pages 48-50.

BOEHM'S CHOCOLATES
Visitors may watch Boehm's super-rich chocolates being made. Call for information and reservations. 255 NE Gilman Boulevard, Issaquah.

Phone: 392-6652

BOEING'S EVERETT PLANT
See page 55.

CARNATION FARM
The fabled Carnation's dairy grounds are no
longer open for tours.

CASUAL CABS
Pedicab tours of the Waterfront and Pioneer
Square areas weekends and summer. Cabs are
available near the Aquarium or call 623-2991.
Cost depends on tour and number of passengers.

CHINATOWN DISCOVERY TOURS
An informal guided tour of the International District; tours last two or three hours and some include dim sum lunch or dinner.

Phone: 236-0657

CHRYSLER AIR/SCENIC FLIGHTS
A 20-minute narrated tour over Seattle in a float-
plane. Flights leave from the Chrysler Air dock at
the southeast end of Lake Union, 1325 Fairview
Avenue East; $32.50 a person. Others available to
Mt. Saint Helens, the San Juan Islands, etc.

Phone: 329-9638

EXPLORE SEATTLE
Guided van tours of Seattle or outlying areas.
Prices from $30 depending on destination and
number of people.

Phone   878-3965

FLYWRIGHT HELICOPTER TOURS
Custom helicopter tours depart from this Federal
Way location. Prices vary; call for information.

Phone: 206-838-9141

GRAY LINE TOURS
Tours to several areas are mentioned by area.
Tours depart from the Washington State Conven-
tion and Trade Center. Phone 626-5208.

The Herbfarm

See page 58.

Horse-drawn Carriage Tours

Several operators do leisurely city tours in horse-drawn carriages. Most are 15-20 minutes and are available on the Waterfront, in Pioneer Square, or at Westlake Park afternoons and evenings.

The Kingdome

See page 28.

Lake Cruise

Argosy's Eastside cruise tours the shores of Lake Washington, departing from either Kirkland's Marina Park or Chandler's Cove on Lake Union. Tours are $1\frac{1}{2}$ or 2 hours, depnding on the starting point.

Cost: Adults, $17.61 or $18.59. Children 5-12, $8.04 or $11.09

Phone: 623-4252

The Locks

See pages 39-41.

Pike Place Market

See page 13.

Redhook Ale Brewery

See page 93.

Seattle Tours

Narrated three-hour tours throughout the Seattle area in spacious vans. Includes stops along the way to see the locks and views.

Cost: $30

Phone: 660-TOUR

Seattle Trolley Tours

Trolley buses operated by Gray Line make a loop in the city as drivers point out highlights along the way. Tickets are for all day, allowing passengers to get on and off at will.

Price: Adults $11.90. Students $10.82. Teens $9.74. Children 5-12, $5.41.

SEATTLE WALKING TOUR

Seattle's original walking tour, these two-hour tours walk approximately two miles through the downtown. Guide Duse McLean, author of *The Pocket Guide to Seattle*, emphasises area history and architecture. Tours meet by SBC Coffee in front of Westlake Center Wednesday and Thursday evenings at 5:30pm during the summer and Saturdays at 10:30am. By reservation at other times.

Cost: $10 a person.

Phone: 885-3173

SEE SEATTLE WALKING TOUR

Walking tours covering downtown Seattle and the Waterfront. Depart from Westlake Center mornings and afternoons Tuesday-Saturday, and take 2-3. hours. Other tours available.

Cost: $10-$15 a person.

Phone: 226-7641

SHOW ME SEATTLE

Morning and afternoon van tours of the Seattle area with stops at scenic spots.

Phone: 633-CITY

SPIRIT OF PUGET SOUND

See page 21.

TASTE OF THE NW WALKING TOUR

A 3-hour tour combining walking and shopping at the Public Market, followed by eating the results at the Painted Table restaurant. Wednesdays and Saturdays; reservations required.

Cost $55

Phone: 624-3646

TILLICUM VILLAGE TOURS

See page 20.

UNDERGROUND TOURS

See page 24.

UNIVERSITY OF WASHINGTON CAMPUS

See page 46.

TRAINS

Railroads were critical to Seattle's development in the 19th century, providing a link for commerce between Seattle and the rest of the country. Several grand old trains from earlier days travel scenic routes during the summer months and on some holidays. Call for hours and prices.

The **Snoqualmie Railroad**, operated by the **Puget Sound Railway Historical Association**, runs steam- and diesel-powered trains from depots at North Bend's Railroad Park and the historical station in Snoqualmie. Roundtrip takes approximately $1\frac{1}{4}$ hours. Weekends in the summer; Sunday only in April, May, September and October; plus Christmas trains. Phone 1-206-888-3030 or 746-4025.

The **Spirit of Washington** dinner train travels from Renton north to the Columbia Winery in Woodinville. For more information phone 1-800-876-RAIL.

The **Mt. Rainier Scenic Railroad** departs from the Elbe station east of Tacoma and Hwy 7 for a $1\frac{1}{2}$ hour trip accompanied by live music. Runs daily during the summer and on weekends in September. Phone 1-206-569-2588.

The **Lake Whatcom Railroad** goes through forests and farmlands east of Sedro Woolley for a scenic 11-mile trip. Weekends in the summer plus Christmas trains. Phone 1-206-595-2218.

For a short, scenic trip the **Pt. Defiance, Quinault & Klickitat Railroad** runs an authentic geared logging train through logging exhibits in **Pt. Defiance Park** outside of Tacoma. Weekends in the summer and Christmas trains during the holidays. Phone 1-206-752-0047.

VIEWS AND DRIVES

Seattle is a city of views — of mountains and water, of sunrises and sunsets, on clear days and gray days — there are hundreds of spectacular views. But even on ordinary days, Seattle's natural beauty with its expansive vistas offers many splendid sights.

The following is a list of some good ideas, but everyone has favorites.

The observation deck at the **Space Needle**. See page 31.

The view from the balcony outside the Chinese Throne Room of the **Smith Tower**. See page 25.

Columbia Center — The highest view in Seattle. Check in with the Security Desk at the Fifth Avenue entrance.

Hours:	8:30am-4:30pm, Mon-Fri.
Cost:	Adults $3.50. Seniors & children 7-15, $1.75.
Phone:	386-5147

The view from the back (water) side of **Pike Place Market**.

Victor Steinbrueck Park near Pike Place Market, overlooking Elliott Bay.

From on top of the new Mt. Baker tunnel at the west end of the I-90 floating bridge.

Kerry Park, the small park west of Queen Anne Avenue on Highland Drive with the much photographed Changing Forms sculpture; and a little farther west, **Betty Bowen Park** across from **Parsons Gardens.**

Many of the streets on **Queen Anne**, especially **Olympic Way** and **Highland Drive.**

Kobe Terrace, on Washington Street just west of the freeway in the International District.

José Rizal Park, at 12th Street South and South Judkins, overlooks the Kingdome, Elliott Bay and beyond.

The **University of Washington campus**;

Rainier Vista from **Drumheller fountain.**

Boren Park on 15th Avenue and Garfield Street, northeast of Volunteer Park.

Roanoke Park at the intersection of Roanoke Street and 10th Avenue overlooking Portage Bay.

The Lake Washington floating bridges. (Avoid the commuter hours or you'll have a longer view than you need.)

Volunteer Park. The view from ground is great, but the view from the top of the **water tower** in Volunteer Park is the most panoramic in Seattle; open 7am-8:15pm.

Drive along Lake Washington Boulevard — any of the parks along the way.

Gasworks Park on Lake Union.

Ivar's Salmon House on Lake Union.

Shilshole Marina and **Golden Gardens Park** north of the Locks.

Discovery Park from the paths and down by the **Daybreak Star Indian Cultural Center.**

Magnolia Boulevard: There are several parks and viewpoints along Magnolia Bluff with spectacular views of Puget Sound and the Olympic mountains.

There are several expansive views in West Seattle looking north to Seattle or west across Puget Sound. The **Belvedere Viewpoint** on SW Admiral and SW Olga is on the main road into West Seattle. On the north side, the **Hamilton Viewpoint** at California SW and SW Donald overlooks Elliott Bay. **Alki Beach** runs along the entire northwest side of West Seattle; a statue commemorating the founding of Seattle is on the western end. The **Alki Point Lighthouse** sits on the western tip and farther south along Beach Drive is **Schmitz Viewpoint Park.**

WATER ACTIVITIES

Water, water everywhere — and so many ways to enjoy it. With all the rivers, sloughs, lakes and salt water around Seattle, many activities revolve around the water. Here are some suggestions.

BEACHES

Freshwater: Green Lake in Woodland Park; Seward Park, Madrona Park, and Madison Park on the west (Seattle) side of **Lake Washington**; call the Seattle Parks Department, 684-4075, for information. Several parks along the Lake Washington waterfront in Kirkland and Bellevue on the east side of Lake Washington. Also Sammamish State Park on **Lake Sammamish**. Call the Bellevue Park Department, 462-6046, or the Kirkland Park Department, 828-1218, for information.

Salt water: Alki Beach in **West Seattle**; Golden Gardens north of Shilshole Marina. Also Saltwater State Park south of **Des Moines**. Call the Seattle Parks Department, 684-4075, for information.

BOATS

Paddle a canoe to explore the area around the Arboretum and Foster Island. Canoes and rowboats are available from the **University of Washington Water Activities Center** near Husky Stadium on Lake Washington. Call 543-9433 for information.

The **Northwest Outdoor Center** on Lake Union rents canoes and kayaks and leads water tours of the lakes in the summer; phone 281-9694. Kayaks are available from the **Swallows' Nest**, 2308 Sixth Avenue, phone 441-4100. The **Center for Wooden Boats** at the south end of Lake Union rents many kinds of wooden craft; phone 382-2628. On the north end of Lake Union, **Urban Surf** on Northlake Way rents sailboards; phone 281-7834.

At **Green Lake**, there are canoes, rowboats, paddleboats and sailboards for rent; phone 527-0171.

Windsurfing boards and lessons are available on Lake Union, at Green Lake, and in Kirkland. Check the Yellow Pages for listings.

Seacrest Marina in West Seattle rents motorboats for fishing or exploring in Elliott Bay and the Duwamish River; phone 932-1050. Scuba divers congregate west of the marina.

Sailboats and **powerboats** are available from a number of sources. Check ads in newspapers and local boating papers available at nautical supply shops; also ask yacht brokers on Lake Union and at marinas. For boat charters on Whidbey Island or in the San Juan Islands, check with their visitor information centers.

Several operators have fishing boat charters depending upon the season. Check with local marinas, newspapers, the Yellow Pages, or sporting goods stores for information.

River rafting in wilderness areas is an adventurous way to see some of Washington's most beautiful scenery and, possibly, bald eagles. Several companies operate on both sides of the Cascades; the Seattle and Eastside Yellow Pages have listings under "Rafting."

WINERIES

Most Washington wineries grow their grapes in eastern Washington, in the Yakama/Tri-Cities area, but several wineries are located in or near Seattle and offer free tours and/or tastings to the public. In addition to those listed below, there are several wineries on the Olympic Peninsula, pages 65-68.

CHATEAU STE. MICHELLE
One Stimson Lane, Woodinville

Chateau Ste. Michelle, the state's largest winery, has a traditional-style winery chateau on spacious grounds in Woodinville — a nice spot for a picnic. Food for your picnic is available in the large gift shop, along with books, pillows, etc. It has tours followed by tastings on a drop-in basis daily from 10:30am-4:30pm.

Driving time from Seattle: approximately 45 minutes.

Phone: 488-1133

COLUMBIA WINERY
14030 NE 145th Street, Woodinville

Columbia Winery, one of the state's oldest wineries, is in a striking Victorian manor house across the street from Chateau Ste. Michelle. In addition to Columbia's wines, it also handles Paul Thomas and Covery Run wines. The winery has a gift shop and picnic area and is open daily from 10am-5pm for tastings; tours on weekends. The dinner train, **The Spirit of Washington**, stops here.

Driving time from Seattle: approximately 45 minutes.

Phone: 488-2776

E.B. FOOTE WINERY
9354 Fourth Avenue South, Seattle

This tiny winery in the South Park area is operated by its two owners. Open for tastings most Saturdays and Tuesday and Thursday evenings.

Driving time from Seattle: approximately 20 minutes.

Phone: 763-9928

FACELLI WINERY
16120 Woodinville-Redmond Road, Woodinville

This small family-owned-and-operated winery is in a industrial park around the corner from Columbia and Ste. Michelle wineries. It is open for tours and tastings most Saturday and Sunday afternoons; it's a good idea to call first.

Driving time from Seattle: approximately 45 minutes.

Phone: 488-1020

HEDGES CELLARS
1105 12th Avenue NW, Suite A-4, Issaquah

Hedges' tasting room not far from Gilman Village is open for samples of its wines Monday through Saturday from noon-6pm.

Driving time from Seattle: approximately 30 minutes.

Phone: 391-6056

SILVER LAKE SPARKLING CELLARS
17721 132nd NE, Woodinville

This informal winery is just off the SR 522 exit to Woodinville a few miles from Chateau Ste. Michelle. There's a tasting room and gift shop; also a picnic area located beside a shady stream. It is open daily from noon-5pm for tours and tastings of its wines and cider.

Driving time from Seattle: approximately 45 minutes.

Phone: 1-206-486-1900

SNOQUALMIE WINERY
1000 Winery Road, Snoqualmie

Snoqualmie Winery's spectacular location overlooking the Snoqualmie Valley is just off the eastbound Snoqualmie Falls exit, #27, on I-90. Open for tours, tastings and picnics 10am-4:30pm daily.

Driving time from Seattle: approximately 40 minutes.

Phone: 1-206-392-4000

OTHER SOURCES OF INFORMATION

There is excellent information about Seattle available from many sources; some are supported by their membership or advertisers. The following is a list of resources.

The **Seattle/King County Convention and Visitors Bureau,** known as the SKCCVB or The Bureau:

The executive offices are in the 520 Pike Building, Suite 1300, Seattle,WA 98101. Phone: 461-5800.

The **Visitor Information** office is on the Galleria level of the **Washington State Convention and Trade Center**, located between Union and Pike Streets at Eighth Avenue. Phone: 461-5840.

The Information Booth at Seattle Center is across from the Monorail ramp, open summer only. Phone: 461-4244.

The Bureau publishes several booklets: Its comprehensive *Events Calendar* lists Seattle's attractions and events for the four to six months covered by the booklet; it also publishes a *Visitors Guide* and a *Lodging Guide*.

The Bureau will mail out requested information — it has an abundance of material about Seattle and Washington.

The staff at the **Information Desk** on the main floor of **Westlake Center** provides general visitor information and can make hotel and entertainment arrangements. Phone: 467-1600.

There are computerized information kiosks in many hotels, lobbies and at the airport.

The **East King County Convention and Visitors Bureau** is located just west of I-405 from Bellevue's NE Fourth Street exit, at 520 112th Avenue NE Suite 101, Bellevue, WA 98004. It has staff to answer inquiries and publishes the *East King County Visitors Guide,* a quarterly booklet about Eastside attractions. Phone: 455-1926.

The **South King County Convention and Visitors Bureau** serves the area south of Seattle from two locations: 15030 8th Avenue SW, Burien, and 16400 Southcenter Parkway, Suite 20, at Southcenter Mall. Phone: 1-800-638-8613.

The **Washington State Department of Tourism** publishes three seasonal *Field Guides*, which have information for the state with the locations and phone numbers of the various visitor information centers. They also publish the Washington State Lodging & Travel Guide. Phone 1-800-544-1800 for free copies; allow three to four weeks for delivery.

The *Guest Informant*, available in many hotel rooms, emphasizes shopping opportunities in and around Seattle. A smaller *Quick Guide* is available at visitor information centers.

Where magazine, published monthly, covers current events and things to do in the Seattle area. It's free and available from Visitor Information desks and concierges.

The Greater Seattle Business Association publishes the *GSBA Guide* of businesses serving the Gay and Lesbian community. The *Guide* is available at many shops along Broadway or call 443-4722.

Access Seattle, produced in 1988 by the Junior League and Easter Seal Society, is a guidebook for people with handicaps.

The folks at Seattle Public Library's **Quick Info Line** will answer almost any question thrown at them. Phone: 386-4636.

The Seattle Arts Commission booklet, *Seattle's Public Art*, is a guide to the many public works of art in and around Seattle. See Art section, page 89.

NEWSPAPERS

The Thursday, Friday and Saturday editions of

The Seattle Times, the *Seattle Post-Intelligencer* (known as "The PI") and the suburban papers have timely and extensive information about current happenings as well as restaurant reviews. Thursday's PI has a Travel and Outdoor section called Getaways with a Calendar of Events for the following week, while Thursday's Times has Tempo with extensive information about entertainment, music, visual arts, and restaurant reviews.

There are also several free papers: *The Weekly* has excellent current events information, especially about the arts, and *Eastside Week* has information about goings on the the Eastside; *Downtown Source* covers Seattle events and issues; The *Stranger* covers the fringe scene; and the *Rocket* emphasizes Seattle's music.

Seattle's Child has a monthly calendar that lists a wide variety of events for children and families.

Seattle Gay News is a weekly newspaper covering gay/lesbian happenings in the Seattle area.

In addition, there are many booklets and other materials put out by groups and areas with information pertaining to their area or activities, such as *The Guide to the San Juans* or *The Olympic Peninsula*. The local areas' chambers of commerce and visitor information centers are excellent sources for up-to-date information.

FOREIGN LANGUAGE INFORMATION

Some foreign language brochures and guide books, such as the *Pacific Companion* (Japanese) are available at SKCCVB Information Centers, page 131.

The Visitor Information Booth by baggage carousel #1 at Sea-Tac Airport is staffed by Japanese-speaking personnel; open 9:30am-1:30pm daily (hours may change to accommodate airline schedules). Phone 433-4679.

Several countries have Consulate offices in Seattle; for information, call the Consulates.

GLOSSARY

Every area has its idioms that locals use but baffle visitors and newcomers. Here's a glossary to understanding the words and customs of the Northwest's largest city.

ALKI *pronounced "Alk-eye"* 1. Means "bye-and-bye" in Chinook jargon. Name given to the first settlement (now part of West Seattle) where the pioneering Denny Party settled. The full name was "New York Alki," reflecting settlers' dreams that this would someday be the New York of the West. 2. Official state motto of Washington.

BALLARD Scandinavian enclave on the north side of the ship canal where residents eat lutefisk and say "Ya, sure, you betcha."

BELLTOWN Area on the north side of downtown, which includes First, Second and Third Avenues in the Regrade, with lots of new condos and trendy restaurants. Originally William Bell's claim.

BICYCLE COPS Hardy police who patrol Seattle's streets and alleys. Seattle's was the first police force to use bicycles. It was so successful other cities copied the idea.

BILL GATES 1. Founder and head of Microsoft, a computer software company. 2. The richest, or second richest, man in the United States. 3. Owner of a seven-acre spread on Lake Washington that someday will become a 40,000 square-foot dream house for him and his family.

BROADWAY The main street in the Capitol Hill area; known for its eclectic shops, bars and people.

BUCKY'S Name of a bicycle delivery service, whose strong-legged messengers started the grunge style of layered dressing.

Now used as a verb: "I'll Bucky it over to you."

CAPITOL HILL Area east of downtown with residents of many lifestyles. Named after an area in Denver by the developer or because supporters wanted Seattle to be the state capitol.

COUNTERBALANCE Refers to the old streetcar counterbalance on the flat part of Queen Anne Avenue North; may also mean the street itself.

DAMP Just short of wet. What the ground, buildings and trees are.

DAWGS Because the University of Washington's mascot is a husky, its athletic teams are known as the dogs or dawgs; i.e., "Dawgs thrash Cougs." May also mean a student at the university.

DOME Much maligned large concrete hulk at the south end of town, where nobody wants to play anymore. Enhanced by a white slug cozied up to its backside.

DRY SPELL Period of 24 hours without rain.

EMERALD CITY The Convention and Visitors Bureau came up with this nickname for our city so sportscasters could say "We're here in the Emerald City..." Replaced the previous "Queen City."

ESPRESSO Strong, dark coffee used to make lattes. Not EXpresso.

GEODUCK *pronounced "GOO-ee-duck"* A monster clam that lets it all hang out at some fish stalls in the Market.

GRAY The color of the sky when the sun isn't out. There are many subtle variations in grays; some of the more common are: pearl gray, bright gray, battleship gray, dark gray, ominous gray, steel gray, luminescent gray, and slightly gray. It takes years to appreciate the nuances of Seattle's gray skies. A true Seattleite likes them and gets edgy if the sun shines more than two days in a row.

GRUNGE 1. Type of loud music played by groups with names like Mudhoney and Gashuffer. 2. Clothing or style of dress worn by people at grunge concerts.

HERSCHEL The generic name given to the voracious sealions that prey on salmon outside the fish ladder at the locks.

HILLCLIMB The thousands (actually 158) of steps linking the Pike Place Market on First Avenue with the Waterfront. Flanked by shops and restaurants along the side for those who need an excuse to stop along the way.

HONK Don't do it; just wait. A discrete light beep is OK to greet a friend.

IVAR'S Seafood restaurants founded by Ivar

Haglund, who was known for his puns ("keep clam") and his offbeat promotions.

JAYWALK Another no-no. Seattle police give tickets to lawbreakers who cross the street on a red light or in the middle of a block. Guilty jaywalkers will be subject to an astounding $38 fine.

KING COUNTY Most of the greater Seattle area is located in King County, which stretches westward from the Cascade mountains to the east side of Puget Sound. Originally named after U.S. vice president William R. King (who died before taking office); renamed in honor of Martin Luther King. King County has about 1.6 million people.

LAKE Although there are many lakes in the area, "the lake" always refers to Lake Washington, which is Seattle's eastside boundary. About 23 miles long, 50 miles around, and 200 feet deep, it's spanned by three floating bridges, which provide glorious views to drivers stuck on them.

LATTE *pronounced "La-TAY"* A ubiquitous drink served at sidewalk stands, convenience stores, and fancy restaurants. Made with espresso coffee and varying amounts of steamed milk. How you order a latte shows whether you're "in" or not.

LAZY B Affectionate name for Boeing, reflecting the hard-driving work ethic down on the ranch.

MICROBREW Before Seattle was known for its coffee, it was famous for its many microbreweries, which produce distinctive, old fashioned brews.

MOSS Ubiquitous green plant that grows on buildings, sidewalks, and trees. Don't try to tell which way is north by looking at a tree trunk — it'll have moss all over.

MOUNTAIN 1. Refers to Mount Rainier, used as "The Mountain is out." 2. Refers to the weather: if The Mountain is out, it's a clear day. 3. A salutation on good days: "Hey, The Mountain is out."

NEEDLE 1. Locals' term for the Space Needle, symbol of the 1962 World's Fair, which is visible from almost anywhere. 2. Great place for draping inflated giant gorillas or crabs to publicize an event; 3. The most expensive elevator ride in Seattle.

NORDYS Short for Nordstrom, a money-gulping store founded in Seattle. Synonyms: great service, success, stylish.

PASS Refers to Snoqualmie Pass, an hour's drive east of Seattle on I-90. At an elevation of 3000 feet, it is the lowest pass through the Cascades. It also may mean the ski areas at the pass, where the snow is known as Cascade concrete.

PIKE PLACE MARKET Seattle's beloved public market (see page 13); a Seattle institution. Note: This is a tricky term that separates outsiders from the locals. It is "The Pike Place Market," "Pike Place" or "The Market." It is NOT "Pike's Market" or "The Pike Street Market."

PONCHO An acronym for Patrons Of Northwest Civic, Cultural and CHaritable Organizations, which throws a fancy auction to raise tons of money for arts organizations.

PUGET SOUND Not one of the grunge bands, this is the body of water connecting the Pacific Ocean with Elliott Bay. Named, as most things in the area were, by Captain George Vancouver when he explored the Northwest in 1792.

PUYALLUP *pronounced "pew-AL-up"* The Western Washington State Fair, held every September in the town of the same name. Used as "We're going to do the Puyallup."

QUARTERS Neccessity for anyone parking at a street meter in downtown Seattle where one quarter may buy 3 seconds to 30 minutes.

QUEEN ANNE Hill on the north side of down-

town and Seattle Center with spectacular views of Elliott Bay.

QUEEN CITY Seattle's first nickname, dreamed up by a promoter who thought people would like the regal gracious feeling of the Northwest. Fell out of favor in the 1980s.

RAIN Seattle's weather. Outsiders think it rains all the time in Seattle; Seattleites say it hardly ever rains, it just mists or drizzles or is foggy. Whatever it's called, there's about 35 to 40 inches a year, depending on the part of town you're talking about. Not surprisingly, the official rainfall recorder is at Sea-Tac airport, which is one of the driest spots in the area.

RECYCLE With Seattle's enthusiasm for recycling it's important to have conspicuous containers for segregated trash (paper, aluminum, glass, etc.). It's equally important to use products made of recycled materials.

REGRADE Officially "the Denny Regrade," it is the flat area between the downtown core and Seattle Center that was originally Denny Hill. Regraded into a flatland in the early 1900s by overzealous engineers who sluiced the 190-foot hill into Elliott Bay.

SAM Acronym for the Seattle Art Museum, the area's premier art museum with two locations, one at First Avenue and University where Hammering Man exercises; the other, at the original location in Volunteer Park, is the Seattle Asian Arts Museum, or SAAM.

SEATTLE Named for the kindly Indian chief who befriended the first white settlers in this area. The chief's name was more like "Sealth," which was difficult to pronounce, so it was altered slightly to "Seattle." The name replaced the original Indian name "Duwamps," which the settlers thought not grand enough for the great city they envisioned.

SEATTLE TUXEDO Waterproof or denim jacket, plaid flannel shirt, and jeans, worn with sneakers or hiking boots. Appropriate for any occasion.

SLOUGH *pronounced "slew"* Slow running rivers that meander between lakes or saltwater.

SLUG Snail without a shell that thrives in the damp northwest climate. The world's biggest are natives of the Olympic Penninsula.

SONICS Short for "SuperSonics," Seattle's fast-moving basketball team. Also known as the Supes.

SPOTTED OWL Rare owl that lives in old growth forests; an endangered species. Has become the symbol of preservationists.

STREET PEOPLE Politically correct term for people who hang out on sidewalks and ask for money. Often accompanied by dogs.

TACOMA DOME Blue-hued wooden dome on the northern outskirts of Tacoma where rock stars and ice skaters perform.

TACOMA, MOUNT The original name of Mount Rainier, although the pronunciation was probably closer to "Tahoma." Thought to have meant loosely "big white thing over there."

TROLLEY Cheerful green and yellow streetcars along the Waterfront. The streetcars were purchased from Australia after a long campaign by city councilman George Benson who wanted to build a fun train with loud bells.

TUNNEL 1. Refers to the passage under Third Avenue where the super-expensive Metro buses travel if all goes well. 2. A one-of-a-kind civic art program where local artists worked with engineers to make the daily commute an art experience. Also known as the bus tunnel.

U-DUB. Short for the University of Washington, where the top scholars in the state go to cheer on their football team. Syns: UW, U of W.

UMBRELLA 1. Item carried by tourists because

they've heard it rains all the time. 2. Item not carried by locals because it hardly ever rains.

UNDERGROUND 1. Area under the streets in Pioneer Square where the buildings' original lower floors are. The area was covered up when the level of the streets was raised at the turn of the century. 2. An irreverant tour of the area started by a civic booster in the 1970s. 3. Not the bus tunnel.

UNIVERSITY 1. Another way of referring to the U-Dub. Although there are six state universities in Washington, only the University of Washington is known as THE university. 2. Also known as "The U."

VIADUCT Officially known as The Alaskan Way Viaduct, this unsightly, but efficient roadway blocks the city from the waterfront. It can be a road to nowhere for unsuspecting drivers who get on it by mistake and can't get off till the next county.

INDEX